# Copyright Page

Mission to Systems™

Building Institutions That Endure



First Edition
Printed in the United States of America

ISBN: 978-0-9860230-5-7 (Paperback)
ISBN: 978-0-9860230-6-4 (Digital Edition)

Publisher:
Sylvester Renner
Johnson City, Tennessee
www.missiontosystems.com
sylrenner.com

*Companion course available at www.missiontosystems.com*

---

# Dedication

For those who refuse to let good intentions collapse under weak structure.

For founders who carry both vision and burden.

For board members who choose stewardship over status.

And for every child, family, and community whose future depends not just on mission — but on institutions that endure.

---

# Acknowledgments

This book is the result of lived experience — shaped by decades of leadership, challenge, refinement, and learning.

I am deeply grateful to the board members, staff, volunteers, partners, and supporters who walked through seasons of growth and strain alongside me. Governance conversations that felt difficult in the moment became turning points in institutional maturity. Financial discipline that felt tedious became credibility. Written records that felt administrative became protection.

Special thanks to Dr. Brian, whose consistent counsel and encouragement over the years have been unequalled. His investment in me as a person — not only as a leader — has made me better at both.

I owe a personal debt of gratitude to my late father, Rev. Dr. Eustace L. Renner, whose example of service and quiet leadership shaped my understanding of responsibility long before I understood governance. His influence continues to guide my approach to stewardship.

And to my mother, Zain L. Renner, whose enduring support has never wavered.

To the donors and partners who trusted Develop Africa across twenty years — your confidence created accountability. Your questions strengthened structure. Your support made discipline necessary.

And to the founders building today — this framework is offered not as critique, but as protection. May your mission outlast your exhaustion.

— Sylvester Renner

# Epigraph

Things fall apart quietly when systems are absent.
when systems are absent.

— Sylvester Renner

# Preface

Most nonprofit organizations begin the same way: with a mission, a burden, and a founder willing to act.

Someone sees a need others have overlooked or accepted as inevitable. Something in them refuses to ignore it. They start small — often with little funding, limited structure, and a great deal of personal commitment.

Passion fuels the early years. Improvisation fills the gaps.

Decisions are made quickly, responsibilities overlap, and progress depends heavily on the founder's energy, judgment, and relationships.

This stage is natural. In fact, it is often necessary. Mission precedes structure.

But over time, many organizations reach a turning point.

Growth introduces complexity. Programs expand. Donors expect transparency. Staff multiply. Partnerships increase. Decisions carry larger consequences.

What once worked — intuition, personal oversight, and informal systems — begins to strain under the weight of scale.

This is the moment when many founder-led organizations encounter what I call the structural plateau.

The mission remains strong. The need remains urgent. But the organization's structure has not yet evolved to support the impact it seeks to achieve.

This book is about navigating that transition.

It explores how organizations move from mission-driven beginnings to durable institutions — organizations capable of sustaining their work beyond the energy and presence of any single founder.

The ideas in this book come from nearly two decades of building and leading a nonprofit organization working across borders. Operating in multiple countries introduces additional layers of complexity: distance from programs, regulatory differences, cultural translation, financial oversight challenges, and logistical hurdles.

In such environments, weak systems reveal themselves quickly. Structures must be clear. Processes must be repeatable. Governance must be intentional.

But while the examples in this book often draw from cross-border nonprofit work, the frameworks themselves apply to any founder-led organization.

Whether an organization operates in one city or across continents, the underlying challenge is the same: How does a mission-driven initiative become a stable institution? How does an organization preserve its passion while building the structure necessary for long-term impact?

This book offers practical frameworks to help answer those questions.

It is not a theoretical manual. It is a field guide drawn from lived experience — successes, mistakes, and the gradual lessons that emerge when a mission grows into an organization.

My hope is that these ideas will help founders, leaders, and boards build organizations that are not only effective today, but durable for decades to come.

Because mission starts the work. But systems sustain it.

# The Mission to Systems Doctrine

The ideas in this book can be summarized in five principles that govern institutional durability.

Mission begins the work.
Structure stabilizes it.
Systems sustain it.
Governance protects it.

The Mission to Systems Transition

Evidence proves it.

Every durable institution moves through this progression.

Passion may launch the work, but institutions endure only when structure, systems, and governance mature alongside the mission.

The chapters that follow examine how that transition occurs in practice.

# Author's Note (From the Founder)

I didn't start a nonprofit with a master plan.

What I had was a problem I couldn't stop thinking about and a conviction that I needed to act. On January 30, 2006, Develop Africa was officially incorporated with the State of Tennessee as a nonprofit organization. I had never run an organization before.

Over the last two decades I've lived nearly every phase of nonprofit leadership — the excitement of early wins, the frustration of systemic constraints, the cost of moving too fast without enough structure, and the slow satisfaction of building something that begins to function on its own.

That experience is what this book is made of. Not theory. Not borrowed frameworks. The specific lessons that emerged from specific decisions — some wise, some costly, all instructive.

Working across countries and cultures added dimensions that domestic nonprofit literature rarely addresses: distance from programs, regulatory differences, cultural translation, and the discipline required to maintain accountability from thousands of miles away. Those pressures sharpened everything in this guide.

This is the book I wish someone had handed me before I filed my first form, recruited my first board member, or raised my first dollar. Use it accordingly.

— Sylvester Renner

# How to Use This Book

This book is organized around a journey that most founder-led organizations share: beginning with a problem worth solving, building the structures that allow the work to grow, and navigating the transition from a personality-driven organization to one that can endure beyond any single leader. The frameworks in these pages apply wherever that journey unfolds — across sectors, geographies, and organizational types. Use them at the stage you are actually in.

You may be a founder at the early stages of formation, still deciding whether to incorporate and how. You may be an executive director whose organization has grown faster than its governance. You may be a board member who suspects something structural is missing but lacks the language to name it. You may be a funder or program officer whose grantees struggle with the governance gaps this book addresses. You may be leading an organization with programs in multiple locations — across states, across borders, or across both. Wherever you are, the frameworks here are drawn from real conditions and designed to apply to yours.

Whoever you are, this book is organized to meet you at your current stage of institutional development.

## Founder-Centric Stage — Building the Foundation:

Read Chapters 1 through 4 first. These address the foundational decisions — whether to incorporate, how to structure legally, what a functioning board actually requires — that shape every decision that follows. The single most expensive mistake an early-stage founder makes is treating formation as administrative rather than architectural. These chapters address that mistake before it compounds.

## Structured Stage — Formalizing What Works:

Start with Chapters 5 through 9. You have structure in place but may be discovering that structure does not yet function the way you imagined. Boards that exist on paper but not in practice. Financial systems that are documented but not disciplined. Programs that are real but not yet evaluated. These chapters address the gap between having structure and having structure that works.

## Institutional Stage — Designing for Durability:

Chapters 10 through 13 speak most directly to your season. Governance that has accumulated rather than been designed. The founder's role evolving from operator to architect. The structural readiness required before growth. The sustainability questions that resource growth cannot answer. These chapters are about moving from structure that exists to structure that endures.

The setting may differ. The structural principles do not.

Whether you are building a nonprofit in a single city, a startup, a social enterprise, or a growing organization of any kind, the underlying challenge is the same: how to move from founder-driven effort to an institution that can endure.

Most of the examples in this book come from work across countries and cultures. But this is not a book about geography. It is a book about structure.

## In Crisis or Transition:

Chapter 13 on founder risk and Chapter 12 on scaling readiness are the most useful for immediate organizational pressure. Chapter 9 addresses what happens when key personnel leave. Chapter 7 addresses financial discipline under strain. Read what is most urgent, then return to the sequence when the immediate situation has stabilized.

## Operational Complexity — Multi-Site or Distributed Work:

The entire book applies. Pay particular attention to the sections on partner relationships (Chapters 5 and 14), governance across distributed teams, and the stages of the Governance Maturity Continuum™ that apply when structure must hold across geography, time zones, or regulatory environments.

## A Note on Sequence

The chapters build on each other deliberately. Mission clarity precedes legal formation. Legal formation precedes governance structure. Governance structure precedes financial discipline. Financial discipline precedes fundraising strategy. Fundraising strategy precedes scaling. Each layer requires the layer beneath it to be stable before it can hold weight.

This is not theory. It is the pattern that twenty years of institutional development — documented in this book — actually produced. The sequence exists because the consequences of skipping steps were real.

Do not jump to fundraising before the structural layers beneath it are in place. The sequence exists because skipping steps has consequences — and the consequences compound.

## How to Use the Frameworks

Each chapter in this book contains a named framework — the Mission-Vision-Values Alignment™, the Board Governance Spectrum™, the Financial Transparency Stack™, and others. These frameworks did not precede the experience. They emerged from it. The Mission-Vision-Values Alignment exists because I learned, during the Dream Again Home crisis, what happens when an organization responds to urgent need without asking whether the response is within its mission. The Founder Continuity Spectrum exists because I spent years in Stage 1 without recognizing I was there. The frameworks are maps drawn after the territory was walked.

Use them as diagnostic tools, not checklists. The question is not whether your organization has a mission statement. It is whether that mission statement has ever been the deciding factor in a hard institutional choice. The question is not whether you have a board. It is whether your board governs or merely exists.

Apply the frameworks honestly. The gap between where your organization is and where these frameworks suggest it should be is not a failing. It is a starting point. Every organization represented in this book — including Develop Africa — spent years at stages it had not yet named. Naming the stage is the beginning of addressing it.

This book will not eliminate risk, simplify governance, or make leadership effortless. It will make fragility visible — and visibility creates discipline. Do not rush through the material. Return to the Governance Maturity Model annually. Revisit the Structural Plateau warning before every major expansion.

---

## From the Field: The Minutes That Changed Everything

For the first five to eight years of Develop Africa's existence, we had a board in the way that many early-stage nonprofits have a board: names on a document, people who believed in the mission, occasional conversations. What we did not have were regular meetings, consistent minutes, or the structural habits that transform a board from a governance requirement into an actual governance body.

Part of this was geography. Janet was based in Sierra Leone. George eventually returned to Kenya and communication faded. Henry traveled frequently. In an era before reliable video conferencing, coordinating meetings across time zones required effort we were not consistently generating. So I consulted with board members individually. It felt like governance. It was not.

The first board meeting that felt genuinely real — where we were all present, where minutes were formally recorded, where we reviewed financials — was around 2014. I can verify this because the minutes exist. Those 2014 records show a board discussing a delay in filing the Form 990, the need to keep QuickBooks updated, what specific actions were required to bring our compliance current. These were not visionary conversations. They were accountability conversations. And they felt different from anything we had done before.

What changed between 2006 and 2014 was not a single dramatic moment. It was accumulation. The departure of Grace in 2012 had forced us to write our first real SOP. The growth in our budget — from $60,000 in 2011 to $181,000 in 2014 — created financial complexity that informal oversight could no longer absorb. The

Dream Again Home in 2014 introduced governance questions that needed real board deliberation.

The honest lesson is that governance does not suddenly arrive. It accumulates through repeated practice: through meetings that happen even when inconvenient, through minutes that exist even when imperfect, through financial reviews that happen even when the numbers are uncomfortable.

We arrived at real governance gradually, under pressure, later than was ideal. That timeline is common. It is also preventable.

Preventing that timeline does not require a dramatic governance overhaul. It requires three specific commitments made early and kept consistently.

First, meet on a schedule — not when it is convenient, but when the calendar says to. A board that meets quarterly under favorable conditions has not yet been tested. The discipline is visible only when meeting is inconvenient.

Second, keep minutes for every meeting, however brief. Not because they are legally required — though they often are — but because minutes are the only proof that governance happened. A board that deliberates without a record has no institutional memory of its own decisions.

Third, review financial reports at every meeting. Not summaries. Not verbal updates. Actual reports, reviewed by people who understand what they are reading. If board members lack financial literacy, that is a training priority, not a reason to defer oversight.

Governance accumulates through these repeated acts. Not through visionary board retreats or ambitious governance redesigns. Through meetings that happen. Minutes that exist. Numbers that get read.

## For Funders and Board Members Reading This

If you are a funder, foundation officer, or board member, this book is for you as much as it is for the founder. These frameworks are not just tools for running organizations. They are lenses for evaluating them.

When you see an organization with clear problem compression, documented systems, and transparent governance, you are looking at institutional readiness. When you see the opposite—founder dependency, unclear processes, informal governance—you are looking at structural risk.

This book teaches you to recognize the difference. And to know which organizations are positioned to sustain progress.

## Speaking With Authority: Boardroom Language

Use this language to communicate more precisely with your board, donors, and team:

**Instead of:** We are growing fast

Say: We are managing complexity at scale

**Instead of:** Everything depends on me

Say: We have a structural dependency we are addressing

**Instead of:** We feel disorganized

Say: We have reached a structural plateau

**Instead of:** We need better people

Say: We need documented systems

**Instead of:** This is a program issue

Say: This is a governance issue

# Table of Contents

# Chapter 1 — Start With the Problem, Not the Organization

There is one structural decision that determines whether your nonprofit will drift, stall, or endure:

**What exact problem are we solving?**

Not the cause.
Not the passion.
Not the aspiration.

The problem.

Every durable institution begins with a clearly defined tension in the world that it exists to resolve.

Ambiguity at this stage is not harmless.
It compounds.

For example, an organization begins focused on "education" but over time adds nutrition, infrastructure, and emergency response. Each expansion responds to real need. None are aligned. The result is scattered rather than strategic.

And compounded ambiguity becomes institutional fragility.

---

## The Mission-to-Systems™ Principle

A nonprofit is not built on passion.
It is built on a defined problem that governs decisions.

When the problem is compressed and clear:

- Programs align.
- Governance stabilizes.
- Fundraising becomes strategic.
- Staffing becomes intentional.
- Trade-offs become easier.

When the problem is vague:

- Activity replaces clarity.
- Opportunity replaces strategy.
- Funding replaces focus.
- Board conversations become philosophical.
- Identity becomes unstable.

Most nonprofits do not collapse dramatically.

They stall quietly.

---

## The Problem Compression Principle

Strong institutions compress broad causes into precise problem definitions.

Broad cause: Education
Compressed problem: Grade 4 students in rural districts cannot read at grade level due to lack of trained reading instructors.

Broad cause: Youth empowerment
Compressed problem: High school graduates lack employable digital skills, leading to underemployment within 12 months of graduation.

Broad cause: Poverty
Compressed problem: Female-headed households in X region lack access to working capital below $500, limiting income stability.

Compression creates governability.

Governance requires something specific to oversee.

Without compression, there is nothing concrete to align around — only aspiration.

---

# The Problem Compression Model™

The model shows how founders move from broad aspiration to governed execution.

Think of it as a funnel that narrows into structural clarity.

---

## How It Works

Problem Compression Model

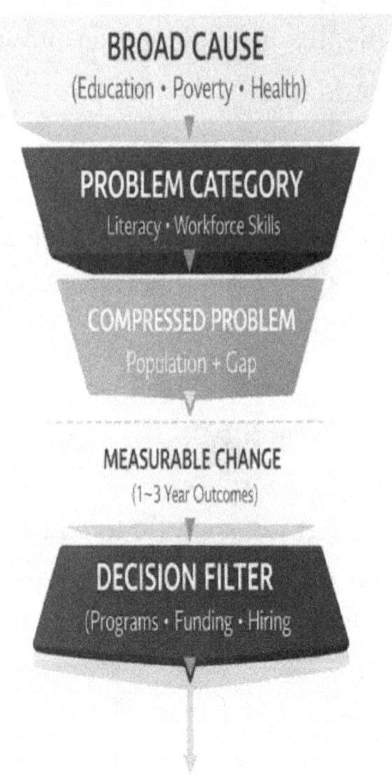


When growth exceeds structure, organizations stall or fracture.

## Level 1: Broad Cause

This is where most founders start.
Example:

- Education
- Poverty
- Youth Empowerment
- Health

Broad causes inspire.
They do not govern.

---

## Level 2: Problem Category

This narrows the field.
Example:

- Literacy
- Workforce readiness
- Access to capital
- Maternal care

Still too broad for governance — but now directional.

---

## Level 3: Compressed Problem

This is the structural core.

It must include:

- Specific population
- Specific gap
- Specific constraint

Example:
"Grade 4 students in rural District X cannot read at grade level due to lack of trained reading instructors."

Now governance can function.

---

## Level 4: Near-Term Change (1–3 Years)

What will measurably shift?

Example:

- 40% increase in reading proficiency among enrolled cohort.
- 60% job placement within 12 months of program completion.

If change is undefined, strategy is undefined.

---

## Level 5: Decision Filter

This is where compression becomes power.

Every major decision passes through this filter:

- Does this program solve the compressed problem?
- Does this funding align with it?
- Does this hire support it?
- Does this partnership strengthen it?

If the answer is no — decline.

That is institutional maturity.

---

The Problem Compression Model illustrates how broad mission energy must be narrowed into a governable core. Compression transforms aspiration into architecture. Without compression, activity expands without alignment. With compression, every decision is filtered through a clearly defined problem, protecting focus and long-term stability.

**From the Field: Isata Kamara**

*Isata Kamara was born in August 1999 in a slum dwelling in Freetown. Her family — six children, two parents struggling to provide — had no reliable access to clean water or electricity. At eleven years old, Isata had not started school. She and her mother sold charcoal to survive.*

*One day, Janet — a coordinator for Develop Africa and a development professional with years of experience in the sector — encountered Isata and her mother selling charcoal in her compound. She asked why the girl was not in school. The answer was simple: her mother could not afford the fees. Janet enrolled Isata in Develop Africa's sponsorship program that same day.*

*Had Janet not acted in that moment, Isata would likely never have gone to school.*

*By 2018, Isata was in her third year of junior secondary school at the Freetown Secondary School for Girls. By 2021, she was preparing to sit the West Africa Senior Secondary School Certificate Examination. Then life intervened. She became pregnant, dropped out, and gave birth to a daughter in early 2024.*

*Develop Africa did not stop. The program team made a welfare visit to her home in April 2024. Isata had resumed her education — this time in cosmetology at a local vocational institute. She completed job training as a prerequisite for graduation. In January 2026, Isata Kamara officially graduated from her cosmetology program. She is now positioned to pursue employment or entrepreneurship in the beauty sector. Over the years, she has also participated in girls' mentoring sessions covering goal setting, financial literacy, self-esteem, and public speaking.*

*Isata's story is not a success story in the simple sense. It is a long-term story — one that includes setbacks, redirections, and hard choices. What made the difference was not a single intervention. It was sustained, patient, long-term support from an organization that did not disappear when circumstances became complicated.*

*That is what institutions do that movements cannot. They stay.*

*Before Frederick's story can be told fully, his mother's must be told first.*

*Olivette was a single parent living on Lewis Street in Freetown with four children and no income. Her husband had left. There was no work. She described her situation simply: "Things were very, very difficult for me. I was a single parent and the father had just left. I had four kids to care for all alone. I was not working. There was nothing going for me."*

*Develop Africa enrolled Olivette in its microfinance program and enrolled two of her children — Frederick and Timothy — in the scholarship sponsorship program. The microfinance loan was interest-free. It gave Olivette capital to run a small shop selling provisions, sachet water, school supplies, and kitchen utensils. The shop generated enough income to provide daily meals and school transportation. The sponsorship program covered school fees, books, pencils, pens, school bags, solar lights, and mosquito nets. Together, the two programs removed every barrier that had been keeping her children from staying in school.*

*She described what this meant in her own words:*

> *"Develop Africa has been of tremendous help to my family. They came in at a time when I had nowhere to turn to. The microfinance loan helped me do some business — a buying and selling business — which I was able to do and then get funds. Out of it I was able to give them lunch and provide feeding for them on a daily basis. What you have done is to transform our lives, to change our story, to give us a brighter destiny."*

*— Olivette, Develop Africa microfinance and sponsorship beneficiary, Freetown*

*Olivette had a dream for her children before things fell apart. She wanted them to become lawyers, doctors, and "renowned personalities in society." That dream had been interrupted by circumstances beyond her control. What Develop Africa provided was not a replacement for that dream. It was the structural conditions that made the dream survivable — the microfinance loan that kept food on the table, the sponsorship that kept the children in school, the computer training that prepared them for what came after.*

*Timothy completed a diploma program in college. Hazel completed secondary school. And Frederick — the boy who enrolled with Develop Africa in Primary Two — graduated with a Bachelor of Science in Geology.*

### Frederick — In His Own Words

*In his own words, after graduation:*

*In 2024 or 2025, Frederick graduated with a Bachelor of Science in Geology. He wants to be a geologist. He is a geologist.*

*He recorded a video message after graduation. His words, unscripted:*

> *"I am very grateful to Develop Africa for all they have done for me throughout my educational journey. I started with them back when I was in Primary Two. They helped me progress from one level to another, throughout my primary, throughout my secondary and even guidance as to what my dreams are, how I can reach my goals to become actually what I want to be — that is a geologist. They even helped me after I took the WASSCE. They enrolled me into the computer program, where I learned how to use the Microsoft Office package, which became of great help to me*

*while I was in college. Now look at me. I am a graduate now. I graduated with a Bachelor of Science in Geology. Glory be to God. I want to bless every single person that is connected, involved in Develop Africa — from the sponsors, to the board, to even the staff. God bless you all. Thank you."*

*— Frederick, Develop Africa beneficiary, Bachelor of Science in Geology*

*Frederick's story and Isata's story are not the same story. Isata's path redirected more than once. Frederick's moved steadily forward. Both were supported by the same organization across more than a decade. Both demonstrate what long-term institutional commitment looks like from the receiving end. Not a single intervention. Not a one-year program. A sustained presence in a child's life, from Primary Two to graduation, from the first pencil to the last exam.*

*That is what Develop Africa was built to do. Not to solve poverty. To do something specific: help children in Sierra Leone stay in school. Frederick stayed. He graduated. He is a geologist.*

*The stories in this book span twenty-three years, two continents, and every stage of organizational life. A girl on a pavement in 2003. A training room with a bedsheet screen in 2006. A nurse who died in 2014 and the twenty-two children she left behind. A building refurbished in crisis that still houses orphans in 2026. A mother who survived on microfinance loans long enough to see her son graduate as a geologist. One hundred thousand pencils placed in ten thousand hands on a single day.*

*Taken individually, each of these is a program story. Taken together, they are an institutional story — what twenty years of governed, documented, accountable mission looks like from the inside.*

*That is what systems make possible. Not any single outcome. The capacity to produce outcomes consistently, across decades, across crises, across the full arc of a child's life from Primary Two to college graduation.*

## Why Founders Resist Narrowing

Founders resist compression for predictable reasons:

- "If we narrow too much, we'll limit funding."
- "There are so many needs — how can we choose just one?"
- "Broad positioning feels bigger."

In early stages, breadth feels strategic.

In mature institutions, breadth without clarity is instability.

Specificity does not shrink opportunity.
It sharpens it.

Trade-offs are not a loss of compassion.
They are the mechanism of focus.

And focus is the mechanism of durability.

---

## The Structural Drift Pattern

When the problem is undefined, this pattern almost always emerges:

1. Activity replaces clarity.
2. Visible need replaces strategy.
3. Funding replaces focus.
4. Board alignment weakens.
5. Identity fragments.

Consider this example:

An organization begins with literacy tutoring.
Within two years, they add:

- Food support
- School supply distribution

- Youth leadership workshops

Each expansion responds to a real need.
Each decision is defensible.

But the original problem was never documented.

When a new board member asks,
"What is our core problem?"
three different answers emerge.

That is not growth.
That is structural drift.

Drift does not feel like failure.

It feels like busyness.

---

## The Funding Distortion Effect

Funding does not create instability.
It exposes it.

A youth job-readiness nonprofit receives a large corporate grant for environmental clean-up programming.

The funding is attractive.
The board approves expansion.

Two years later:

- Staff capacity is fragmented.
- Reporting requirements double.
- Program identity blurs.
- Core outcomes weaken.

Money amplifies clarity.
It also amplifies confusion.

If your problem definition cannot decline misaligned funding, it is not strong enough yet.

---

## The Governability Test

A clear problem statement must pass three tests:

### 1. Replicability Test

Can every board member state it consistently?

### 2. Boundary Test

Does it clearly define what the organization will *not* do?

### 3. Measurement Test

Can progress toward resolution be observed within 1–3 years?

If any test fails, compression has not occurred.

And without compression, governance will drift.

---

## Founder Insight: Clarity Protects You

Many founders believe exhaustion comes from workload.

Often it comes from decision ambiguity.

When the problem is unclear:

- Every opportunity feels urgent.
- Every partnership feels plausible.
- Every request feels morally valid.
- Every funding stream feels necessary.

Clarity reduces cognitive load.

It creates decision boundaries.

Boundaries create sustainability.

Saying "no" does not contradict compassion.

It protects impact.

## From the Field: The Girl on Howe Street

In 2003, I was walking down Howe Street in Freetown, Sierra Leone, when I passed a young girl crouching on the pavement. She wasn't begging from a distance. She was right there, eye-level with the feet of passersby, asking for something to eat.

I had seen poverty before. But something about that moment — the specificity of it, the particular smallness of one child against the indifference of a busy street — refused to leave me. It compressed itself into something I couldn't generalize away.

That image did not make me want to end poverty in West Africa. It made me want to do something specific: help children in Sierra Leone stay in school. Not every child everywhere. These children. This problem. That compression mattered more than I understood at the time.

Three years later, on January 30, 2006, Develop Africa was officially incorporated with the State of Tennessee as a nonprofit. IRS recognition as a 501(c)(3) followed with the Letter of Determination on April 26, 2006. The organization's first scholarship was named the Promise of Hope — a small program, precisely defined, aimed at keeping students enrolled when their families couldn't cover fees.

We did not start with a comprehensive theory of change. We started with a compressed problem: children in Sierra Leone are dropping out of school because their families cannot afford tuition and basic supplies. That sentence governed every early decision. It told us what to fund and what to decline. It kept us from expanding into nutrition programs when hunger surfaced, or into infrastructure when crumbling schools appeared on our radar.
The compression didn't restrict our compassion. It protected our focus — and our focus protected our impact.

That compression — from a broad cause to a specific, governable problem — is the first structural decision your organization will make. Not incorporation. Not hiring. Not fundraising. This. Because every decision that follows will either be governed by a clear problem definition or pulled in different directions by the absence of one.

The practical steps for doing this are in the chapter that follows. Before you read them, sit with the image that started your organization. What specifically moved you? Not the cause — the moment. That specificity is where your problem definition begins.

---

# Practical Implementation: How to Define the Problem

Clarity is not philosophical.
It is structural work.

Here is how to do it.

## Step 1: Define the Specific Gap

Do not name a cause.
Name a failure.

Ask:

- What is broken right now?
- What is not happening that should be happening?
- What measurable gap exists?

If your description relies on buzzwords, it is not precise enough.

---

## Step 2: Identify the Target Population

"Everyone" is not a population.

Define:

- Age range
- Geography
- Socioeconomic condition
- Daily lived reality

If you cannot picture a specific person affected, the problem is still abstract.

---

### Step 3: Define Observable Change (1–3 Years)

Do not describe the world you want in 20 years.

Describe what will be measurably different in the near term.

Examples:

- Increased literacy proficiency
- Reduced unemployment within a defined cohort
- Increased access to defined resources
- Improved completion rates

If you cannot describe change, you cannot measure impact. If you cannot measure impact, trust erodes.

---

## The 30-Second Clarity Test

If you cannot explain the problem you solve in under 30 seconds:

- Your board cannot defend it.
- Your staff cannot align around it.
- Your donors cannot repeat it.
- Your strategy will drift.

People do not rally around organizations.

They rally around clearly defined needs.

---

# Founder Action Blueprint

# The 30-Day Clarity Sprint

Do not rush past this.

Start here: open a blank document and write this sentence stem — "The specific problem our organization exists to solve is…" Complete it in one paragraph. That draft is Week 1.

**Week 1: Draft Compression**

Write a one-paragraph problem statement that includes:

- Specific population

- Specific gap
- Specific consequence

Revise until it is free of jargon.

---

**Week 2: Alignment Review**

Ask:

- Can every board member repeat this consistently?
- Does anyone interpret it differently?
- Where are the hidden disagreements?

Resolve inconsistencies now.

---

**Week 3: Boundary Mapping**

Document explicitly:

- What we will not pursue.
- What funding we would decline.
- What partnerships are outside scope.

Clarity without boundaries is incomplete.

---

**Week 4: Public Articulation Test**

Explain the problem to:

- A donor
- A volunteer
- Someone unfamiliar with your work

If they can repeat it accurately back to you, compression has occurred.

---

# Required Outputs Before You Proceed

You should be able to produce:

1. A one-paragraph problem statement
   (Clear. Specific. Jargon-free.)
2. A one-sentence 1–3 year impact goal
   (Measurable and realistic.)

If you cannot complete these confidently, pause.

Do not:

- File incorporation documents
- Recruit a board
- Apply for grants

- Launch programs
- Design branding

Do not build structure on ambiguity.

---

## Final Reflection

Every major strategic reset in a nonprofit eventually leads back to this question:

What problem are we actually solving?

The strongest institutions are not the fastest to launch.

They are the clearest about the problem they exist to resolve.

Clarity at the beginning is not restrictive.

It is protective.

*With the problem now compressed and defined, the next task is ensuring that the language used to describe your work — mission, vision, and values — is equally precise. Chapter 2 examines how these three statements function as governance instruments, not branding exercises, and how misalignment between them creates the kind of institutional fragmentation that no amount of funding or activity can repair.*

# Chapter 2 — Mission, Vision, and Values

## The Institutional Clarity

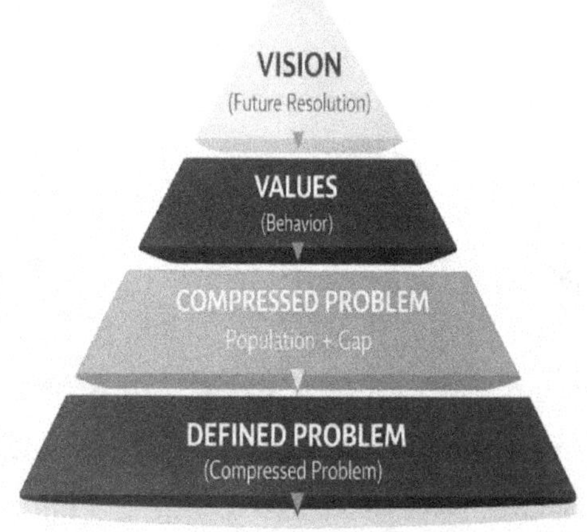


## Framework™

## Core Concept

Problem → governs → Mission
Mission → directs → Activity
Vision → directs → Future Orientation
Values → regulate → Behavior

All three must align — or strain develops.

# Explanation

The Institutional Clarity Framework™ illustrates how problem definition anchors identity. Values regulate behavior. Mission governs present action. Vision directs long-term resolution. When aligned vertically, the institution is stable. When disconnected, fragmentation begins.

Once the problem is compressed, three statements must align:

- Mission
- Vision
- Values

Most organizations treat these as branding exercises.

They are governance instruments.

Together, they form what I call the:

**Institutional Clarity Framework™**

If these three are misaligned, the organization will eventually fragment.

Clarity is not cosmetic.

It is structural.

A stable institution balances mission (what we do now), vision (what we're working toward), and values (how we operate), all anchored to a clearly defined problem.

---

# Mission: The Present-Tense Contract

Mission is not inspiration.

Mission is operational definition.

It answers:

- What do we do?

- For whom?
- To address what defined problem?

Mission must be written in the present tense.

It governs today's activity.

If a mission cannot be used to reject opportunities, it is too vague.

---

## The Mission Discipline Test

A strong mission passes three tests:

### 1. Boundary Test

Does it clearly exclude adjacent but unrelated work?

### 2. Board Test

Can a board use it to approve or reject initiatives?

### 3. Resource Test

Does it guide staffing and budgeting decisions?

If a mission cannot guide resource allocation,
it is ornamental.

---

## Mini-Example: Ornamental vs Operational

Ornamental mission:
"To empower communities to thrive."

Emotionally attractive.
Operationally useless.

Operational mission:
"We provide structured digital skills training to unemployed youth in urban districts to increase employability within 12 months."

The second governs behavior.
The first decorates a website.

Clarity beats cleverness.

---

## Simplicity Is Not Smallness

Many founders overcomplicate mission statements to sound sophisticated.

In reality:

Complexity often hides uncertainty.

The best test:

Can a volunteer, donor, and board member repeat your mission after hearing it once?

If not, simplify.

---

## Vision: The Resolution State

Vision is not what you do.

Vision is what the world looks like if you succeed.

If mission is present tense,
vision is future orientation.

But vision must remain anchored to your problem.

---

## The Vision Anchoring Principle

If your problem is literacy gaps in rural districts,
your vision should not describe global transformation.

Detached vision creates psychological distance.
Anchored vision creates momentum.

Vision must stretch —
but it must stretch proportionally to capacity.

---

## Values: The Behavioral Architecture

Values are the most misused statements in nonprofit governance.

Values are not adjectives.

They are behavioral commitments.

If a value cannot be observed,
it cannot be enforced.

If it cannot be enforced,
it will not survive pressure.

A value like 'integrity' is not an aspirational word. It is a behavioral commitment. How will integrity show up in financial reporting? In difficult conversations? In resisting funding that violates mission?

---

## The Behavioral Definition Rule

Every value must answer:

How does this value change our behavior?

If integrity is a value:
→ Do we report setbacks publicly?

If accountability is a value:
→ Are roles clearly documented and reviewed?

If transparency is a value:
→ Are financial summaries accessible and understandable?

Unenforced values become branding language.

---

→ Appendix E, Tool 07 — Board Values Self-Assessment — provides a structured exercise for translating each of your organization's values into specific behavioral commitments your board can hold itself accountable to. Download at www.missiontosystems.com/tools.

## The Alignment Triangle™

Mission
Vision
Values

These must align like a structural triangle.

If mission shifts but vision remains unchanged, tension emerges.

If values contradict mission execution, credibility erodes.

If vision expands without mission capacity, strain increases.

Alignment stabilizes identity.

---

Visual Framework: The Alignment Triangle

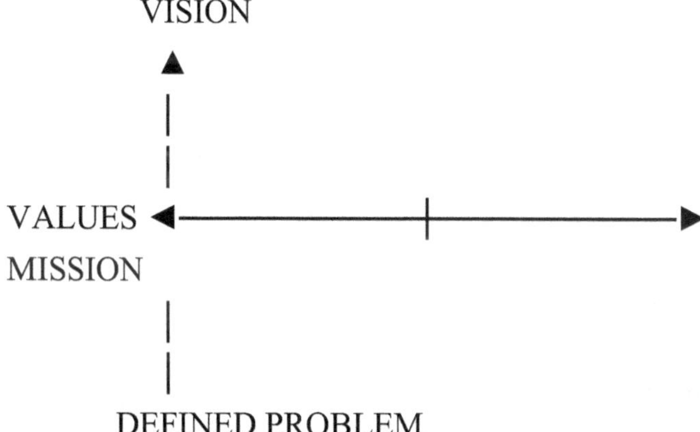


- The Defined Problem anchors the triangle.
- Mission governs present activity.
- Vision guides direction.

- Values regulate behavior.

If any side weakens, structural stability declines.

---

# Practical Construction Guide

Now apply discipline.

## Step 1: Write the Mission

Use this structure:

We provide __________
to __________
so that __________.

Test it against:

- Boundary
- Board
- Resource

If it cannot pass those tests, revise.

---

## Step 2: Write the Vision

Complete:

A future where ______________________.

Or, in two sentences maximum.

Check:

- Does it describe a condition?
- Does it avoid describing organizational growth?
- Does it align with the compressed problem?

---

### Step 3: Define 3–5 Enforced Values

For each value:

- Define observable behaviors.
- Define violations.
- Define operational impact.

If you cannot define behavior, remove the value.

Three enforced values are stronger than seven ignored ones.

---

## Founder Action Blueprint

# The 14-Day Alignment Sprint

### Days 1–3: Draft

Write mission, vision, and 3–5 values.

## Days 4–6: Stress Test

Use the Mission Discipline Test and Vision Anchoring Principle.

## Days 7–10: Behavioral Definitions

Write:

- What this value looks like.
- What violates it.
- Where it applies (board, staff, programs, reporting).

### Days 11–14: Alignment Review

Ask:

- Can leadership repeat all three consistently?
- Do they align with the compressed problem?
- Would we decline funding that violates them?

If misalignment exists, revise.

Do not proceed to structural growth without alignment.

## Required Outputs Before Moving Forward

You should have:

- One operational mission (1 sentence)
- One anchored vision (1–2 sentences)
- Three to five enforced values with behavioral definitions

If these are unclear, pause.

Identity instability precedes governance instability.

---

## Founder Toolkit — Put This Into Practice

You have now defined your mission, vision, and values. Before moving to Chapter 3, translate that clarity into a working document.

Founders who skip this step often discover — under pressure, in a board meeting, or during a funder review — that their stated values do not yet govern their decisions.

→ **Appendix E, Tool 01 — Mission, Vision & Values Worksheet**

Mission explains what you do.

Vision explains why it matters.

Values determine how you behave when pressure rises.

## From the Field: The Dream Again Home

In 2014, Ebola swept through Freetown. A nurse in the Wellington community — a woman who had been part of Ebola sensitization campaigns — contracted the virus at the hospital where she worked. She came home. Her husband contracted it. Both died. Their children, who were already enrolled in Develop Africa's child sponsorship program, were left without parents.

Joshua Sandy, the founder of Door of Hope — our partner organization in Wellington, which has since closed — proposed that we establish an orphanage. Joshua Sandy is one of the most committed community leaders I have encountered in twenty years of this work. His dedication to the children of Wellington — their education, their safety, their futures — long preceded our work together and will continue long after it. Door of Hope existed because Joshua

Sandy saw a need and refused to look away. That is not a small thing. It is the kind of sustained, unglamorous commitment that makes real change possible.and the Dream Again Home had opened. Twenty-one children came to live there.and the Dream Again Home had opened. Twenty-one children came to live there.and the Dream Again Home had opened. Twenty-one children came to live there.

The need for the orphanage was undeniable. We had existing relationships with these children. We had a partner on the ground ready to implement. And through GlobalGiving, we secured a $30,000 grant specifically for emergency response. Within months, a building had been refurbished and the Dream Again Home had opened. Twenty-one children came to live there.

At the time, it felt like the only right thing to do. We were responding to an urgent need.

What we did not fully reckon with was how far outside our mission we had moved.

Develop Africa was built around education: scholarships, school supplies, computer training, keeping children enrolled when families couldn't cover fees. An orphanage is something else entirely. It is residential care — roof, water supply, electricity, daily meals, medical checkups, psychosocial counseling, adolescent health programming, staff oversight, facility maintenance. Our December 2015 board minutes record the specific strain: an inherited unpaid electricity bill from the previous tenants, a shared power meter with a neighbor who was not able to pay his share consistently, a water pump that kept breaking as it was also used by several community members.

These were not program challenges. They were property management problems. We were operating a residential facility with the systems of an education nonprofit.

The harder challenge was mission and organizational alignment. Door of Hope, the implementing organization on the ground, was diligently and faithfully caring for the children every day. We were responsible for operational and living expenses. Over time, we concluded that running an orphanage was not our mission. This was not our strength. We did not have the capacity to manage this long term. We did not have established systems or deep expertise for residential child care. We also struggled to raise the required consistent funding. The Door of Hope team was fully committed to taking care of the kids long term and keeping the home running. Their commitment was laudable. After a long discussion, the Develop Africa board arrived at the conclusion that the children would be better served growing up in families. These were not conflicting values — they were different convictions about what was best for the children.100% responsible for all operational expenses. Over time, we concluded that running an orphanage was not our mission. We did not have established systems or deep expertise for residential child care. We also struggled to raise the consistent funding it required. The Door of Hope team, understandably, had grown deeply attached to the children and to the work they were doing. Their hearts were fully committed to keeping the home running. Ours were pointed in a different direction: we believed the children would be better served growing up in families. These were not conflicting values — they were different convictions about what was best for the children. Bridging that difference while coordinating across two organizations, two countries, and two distinct institutional cultures created the friction that ultimately shaped our exit timeline.

The Develop Africa board convened in August 2017 and concluded that a structured one-year phase-out was the right path forward — deliberate enough to protect the children, and clear enough to give all parties a shared timeline. Over the following year, we executed a phased exit: family tracing, reunification counseling, transition packages for each child, and support for receiving families. By the end of 2018, eighteen of the twenty-two children had been placed with families or adopted internationally. Several families in the United States adopted children from the home. Door of Hope continued supporting the transition of other children into families — which confirmed that family placement had been the right goal all along.into families — which confirmed that family placement had been the right goal all along.into families — which confirmed that family placement had been the right goal all along.

The lesson I carry from the Dream Again Home is not that we were wrong to respond. The nurse who died deserved to have someone step in for her children. But we responded without fully answering the governance question: are we the right organization to carry this, and do we have the systems to do it well?

Mission clarity is not cold-heartedness. It is the discipline that protects beneficiaries from an organization's good intentions outrunning its actual capacity. The Dream Again Home was real and it mattered. It also required years of operational effort and resources that went beyond the education work we were built to do.

The Dream Again Home taught us three things no framework prepares you for.

First, urgency is not the same as readiness. The need was real. The children were real. The $30,000 grant was real. None of that made Develop Africa the right organization to run a residential care facility. A new founder must learn to distinguish between being moved by a need and being equipped to meet it. Those are different questions, and they require different answers.

Second, good values on both sides of a partnership do not eliminate institutional conflict. Joshua Sandy's commitment through Door of Hope to the children was genuine. So was ours. But we had different convictions about what the children needed, different capacities to provide it, and different accountability structures governing our decisions. Written agreements and shared governance frameworks do not remove those differences — but they create a basis for resolving them without damaging the relationship or, more importantly, the people you both serve.

Third, an exit can be as important as an entry. The structured phase-out — family tracing, reunification counseling, transition packages for each child, and support for receiving families — was as deliberate as any program Develop Africa has run. Eighteen of the twenty-two children were adopted into families in the United States. Several families from the Tri-Cities area of Washington State traveled to Sierra Leone, some staying for months to support the children's education while awaiting government approvals and visas. What Develop Africa's structured exit had set in motion — family tracing, transition planning, relationship-building with prospective families — culminated in scenes that no governance document could have predicted: grandmothers near tears in an airport arrivals hall, children carrying balloons, families adding new members across continents.

If your organization is considering expanding into adjacent programs in response to urgent need, ask three questions before you commit: Are we structurally equipped to do this well? Can we sustain the funding this requires? And if we cannot, do we have a plan to exit responsibly?

Compassion without capacity is not kindness. It is risk — to the people you intend to serve.

When mission, vision, and values are precise, they give you language for the hardest moments: this matters, and it is not ours to carry alone. That sentence is easier to say when it is written into your institutional identity — and nearly impossible to say when twenty-two children are standing in front of you.

*There is one more detail worth recording — and it arrived over WhatsApp in April 2026, as this book was being finalized. Joshua Sandy confirmed that the Dream Again Home is still operational. "Dream Again Home is still in operation," he wrote. "More kids come and go" — a phrase that carries its own weight: children arriving as orphans, departing as adopted members of families around* *the world. The full accounting, as Joshua shared it: more than 100 children have passed through the Dream Again Home since it opened in 2015. Forty have been reunified with families in Sierra Leone. Forty-six have been adopted internationally. Ten have received vocational skills training and startup packages to help them build independent lives. The building that Develop Africa refurbished in 2015 — funded by a $30,000 GlobalGiving emergency grant — has now changed the trajectory of over 100 children's lives, and is still running more than a decade later. Develop Africa planted the foundation. Joshua Sandy has continued the work. That is what enduring institutional impact looks like. Not an organization staying forever. An organization building something that continues without it. The goal was never permanence. It was viability.*

*That is what enduring institutional impact looks like. Not an organization staying forever. An organization building something that continues without it. The goal was never permanence. It was viability.*

*Before the mission can be filed, built, or funded, a harder question deserves a serious answer: is a nonprofit the right structure for this work — right now? Chapter 3 examines that question with enough rigor to either confirm your path or redirect it.*

When these three align around a clearly defined problem, structure becomes stable.

When they do not,
no amount of growth will compensate.

*Mission, vision, and values now provide the institutional compass. But before those words are filed with a government agency, a more fundamental question remains: is a nonprofit the right structural vehicle at all? Chapter 3 offers a disciplined framework for evaluating your structural options before committing to the weight of independent incorporation.*

# Chapter 3 — Do You Really Need a Nonprofit?

### The Structural Fit Model™

---

## Structure Follows Function

Before forming a nonprofit, answer a harder question:

**Is a nonprofit structure the correct vehicle for this problem — right now?**

Most founders never ask this question. They assume the answer is yes and file the paperwork. The fact that you are pausing to ask it is the first sign of the discipline this book is building.

Many founders skip this step.

They assume:
If the work is charitable, the structure must be nonprofit.

That assumption creates unnecessary complexity.

Incorporation is not maturity.
It is administrative responsibility.

Structure must serve function.
It must not precede it.

---

## The Structural Fit Model

There are four core structural pathways for mission-driven work:

1. Independent Nonprofit
2. Fiscal Sponsorship
3. Social Enterprise
4. Program Within an Existing Organization

Most founders default to option one.

That is structural haste.

The correct choice depends on:

- Funding model
- Risk exposure
- Administrative capacity
- Governance readiness
- Problem scale

Visual Framework: The Structural Fit Model

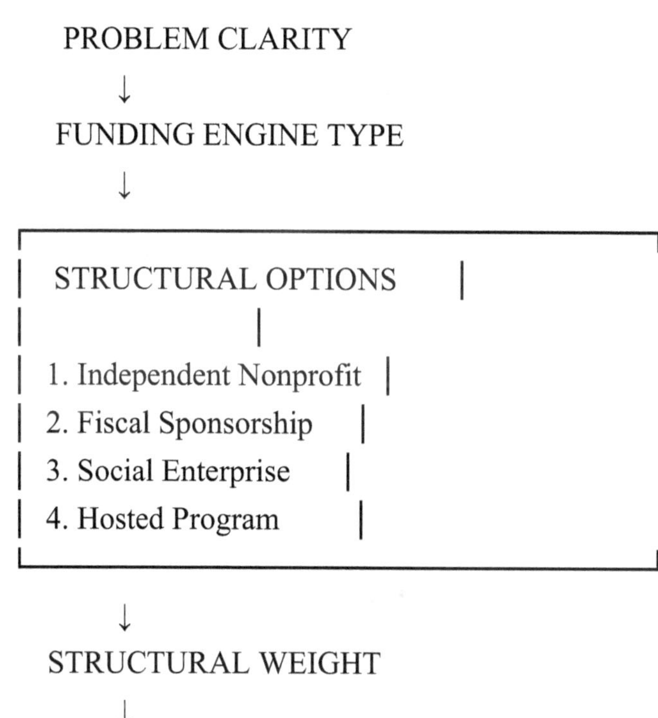


**Interpretation:**

- Clarity determines funding engine.
- Funding engine informs structure.
- Structure carries weight.
- Capacity must match weight.

A nonprofit filing requires annual 990 reporting, board governance written records, conflict-of-interest policies, and compliance calendars.

A fiscal sponsorship requires program reporting but not governance infrastructure. Choose the weight your current capacity can carry.

If weight exceeds capacity, instability follows.

---

# Why Founders Rush Incorporation

Three psychological drivers dominate:

### 1. Legitimacy Signaling

A nonprofit feels official.

### 2. Identity Ownership

Founders want autonomy.

### 3. Funding Assumption

They believe grants require independent status.

Reality:

Legitimacy comes from governance discipline.
Autonomy without systems creates fragility.
Many grants are accessible through fiscal sponsors.

Incorporation does not prove readiness.

It reveals it.

---

## The Structural Weight Principle™

Every structure carries weight.

Independent nonprofit status carries:

- Annual reporting obligations
- Governance documentation
- Financial oversight requirements
- Board management complexity
- Regulatory compliance

If your organizational capacity cannot carry this weight, it will create strain.

Weight without readiness produces instability.

---

## Fiscal Sponsorship: The Maturity Bridge™

Fiscal sponsorship allows you to:

- Raise tax-deductible funds
- Operate under an established 501(c)(3)
- Reduce administrative burden
- Test program viability
- Build systems gradually

## From the Field: What We Didn't Know We Didn't Know

In 2005, I did not know what I did not know.

When my co-founder and I decided to launch Develop Africa, we moved straight into incorporation without questioning the vehicle. We did not ask whether a nonprofit was the right structure. We did not consider alternatives. We simply inquired, learned it was possible, and proceeded.

Part of this was naivety. Part of it was the particular energy that drives anyone who believes they can make a difference — a belief that is often more useful than it is accurate. We had very grand plans. We did not fully understand what it would cost to achieve them. We had not counted the cost.

A coworker told me a story once that has stayed with me. She had given birth to her first child, and when the hospital cleared her for discharge, she looked at the nurse and said: "You are going to allow me to take this baby home? I don't have a clue what I'm doing." She was not joking. She was genuinely unsettled by the weight of something she had chosen but could not yet carry well.

I understood her exactly. That is what it is like to start an organization.

You choose it. You want it. And then you realize, often too late to reverse course, that you did not know what you were committing to. The decision was real but unprocessed. The mission was clear but the cost was not.

If there is anything I would tell a founder sitting where I sat in 2005, it is this: the naivety is not the problem. The naivety is what makes you brave enough to start. The problem is when you never replace it with knowledge. When you keep making decisions the way you made the first one — by instinct, by assumption, without asking the harder question.

This chapter asks the harder question. Answer it honestly before you file anything.

## From the Field: The Question Nobody Asked

In the second half of 2005, my co-founder and I began having serious conversations about how we could make a difference in Africa. We were passionate. We did not have significant resources. And we were, in retrospect, productively naive — naive enough to believe that two people with a clear purpose and no institutional history could start something that would eventually touch thousands of lives.

Around October 2005, we made the decision: we were going to launch Develop Africa. We applied for an EIN with the IRS and received it on December 7, 2005. We opened the organization's first bank account shortly after. Then we began researching how to file for 501(c)(3) status.

We found an organization called the Foundation Group, which helped nonprofits navigate the registration process. Their fee and associated filing costs at the time totaled approximately $1,600. We contracted with them to register with the state of Tennessee and with the IRS, and they helped us draft the original articles of incorporation and the organizational charter. On January 30, 2006, Develop Africa was officially registered. My co-founder played an essential role in assembling the paperwork and driving the process forward. Without that involvement in those early months, the filing would not have happened when it did.

What neither of us asked — what no one told us to ask — was whether a 501(c)(3) was the right structure for what we were trying to do. We did not consider fiscal sponsorship. We did not evaluate whether a giving circle or a community fund accomplishes the same goals with less overhead. The assumption that charitable work requires a nonprofit felt so obvious that it never became a question.

Twenty years later, I believe we made the right call. The work we do requires independent identity, long-term donor relationships, and governance accountability that fiscal sponsorship would not have provided at scale. But I reached that conclusion by accident, not by analysis.

This chapter exists so you do not have to. Choosing structure should be a deliberate act, not a default.

*Chapter 4 treats legal formation not as paperwork to complete, but as the first architectural decision of the institution — one that sets the governance standards, compliance rhythms, and authority structures that will either protect or expose the organization for years to come.*

It creates what I call:

**The Maturity Bridge™**

It allows you to test:

- Problem clarity
- Program model
- Funding patterns
- Governance dynamics

Without carrying full structural weight.

Independence without readiness is fragility.

---

## Social Enterprise as Structural Fit

If your solution generates earned income sustainably, a nonprofit may not be the optimal vehicle.

A social enterprise may provide:

- Greater flexibility
- Faster iteration
- Reduced compliance burden
- Clearer revenue alignment

The structural vehicle must match the funding engine.

Misalignment here creates chronic strain.

---

# Hosted Program Model

Sometimes the fastest and most responsible path is partnering with an existing organization.

This option:

- Avoids duplication
- Leverages mature systems
- Accelerates impact
- Reduces early-stage risk

It requires humility.

But humility often produces durability.

---

# The Governability Threshold™

Before incorporating, confirm:

- The problem is clearly defined.
- Mission is operational and aligned.
- Initial governance partners exist.
- Basic financial tracking is in place.
- Compliance obligations are understood.

If these thresholds are not met, formation should be delayed.

This is not hesitation.

It is discipline.

---

## Structural Comparison Snapshot

| Dimension | Independent Nonprofit | Fiscal Sponsorship | Social Enterprise | Hosted Program |
|---|---|---|---|---|
| Admin Burden | High | Low–Moderate | Moderate | Low |
| Governance Required | Yes | Sponsor-led | Optional | Host-led |
| Speed to Launch | Slow | Fast | Moderate | Fast |
| Autonomy | High | Shared | High | Shared |
| Best For | Proven models | Testing & pilots | Revenue-driven | Early-stage ideas |
| Risk | Overweight structure | Sponsor dependence | Mission drift | Limited control |

There is no “right” structure.

Only the right structure for now.

---

## Founder Action Blueprint

## The Structural Decision Memo (Required Before Filing)

Before incorporation, write a one-page memo addressing:

1. Why this problem requires donations or grants.
2. Why fiscal sponsorship is insufficient (if rejecting).
3. Why earned income cannot sustain the model (if rejecting).
4. What administrative systems are already functioning.
5. What governance capacity exists today.
6. The top 3 risks of incorporating now.

If you cannot write this, you are not ready.

---

## Decision Checklist

Before choosing independent nonprofit status:

☐ Problem is compressed and defined
☐ Mission is operational
☐ Financial tracking exists
☐ At least three governance-ready board candidates identified
☐ Alternatives evaluated seriously
☐ Incorporation is not driven by ego or pressure

If multiple boxes are unchecked:

Pause.

Structure does not create clarity.

Clarity determines structure.

---

## Founder Toolkit — Before You File Anything

This chapter has asked hard questions about whether incorporation is the right choice for you, right now. Before answering yes, your readiness must be scored honestly — not assumed.

The Founder Readiness Index™ operationalizes Chapters 1–3 into a scored assessment. A total score below 24, or any single section below 7, means do not proceed. Pass it first. Then file.

**→ Appendix E — Founder Readiness Scorecard (FRI) | Nonprofit Formation Readiness Gate**

Choosing a structure is not a moral decision.

It is a strategic responsibility.

The strongest founders choose the lightest structure that still allows impact to grow.

Structure should follow demonstrated stability — not ambition.

Ambition without architecture collapses.

*Structure has been chosen. Now it must be built correctly. Chapter 4 examines the legal formation process not as a finish line, but as the beginning of ongoing governance responsibility — and explains why the discipline applied at this stage determines whether the institution develops strength or fragility.*

# Chapter 4 — Legal Formation

## The Formation Discipline Model™ (U.S. Focus)

---

## Legality Is Not Maturity

Incorporation creates legitimacy.

Many founders reach the legal formation stage and feel a sense of arrival — as if the hard part is over. It is not. But the fact that you have made it this far means you have already done something most people who start with a mission never complete.

It does not create discipline.

Filing Articles of Incorporation,
obtaining an EIN,
drafting bylaws,
appointing a board,
and applying for 501(c)(3) status
are necessary steps.

But they are structural containers.

A container without governance is fragile.

Many founders treat formation as the finish line.

It is the starting threshold.

---

## The Formation Discipline Model

Proper legal formation requires five layers of discipline:

1. Structural Clarity
2. Governance Architecture
3. Authority Boundaries
4. Compliance Rhythm
5. Documentation Infrastructure

If any layer is weak, instability compounds later.

---

Visual Framework: The Formation Discipline Model

DOCUMENTATION INFRASTRUCTURE

▲

COMPLIANCE RHYTHM

▲

AUTHORITY BOUNDARIES

▲

GOVERNANCE ARCHITECTURE

▲

STRUCTURAL CLARITY

Interpretation:

- Structural clarity is foundational.
- Governance architecture builds oversight.
- Authority boundaries prevent power confusion.
- Compliance rhythm builds predictability.
- Documentation infrastructure protects continuity.

Each layer is protective. Eliminate one, and the credibility of the entire structure is compromised.

---

# Layer 1: Structural Clarity

Your Articles of Incorporation must reflect:

- Your compressed problem
- Your operational mission
- Your intended charitable purpose

Generic templates create generic identity.

Incorporation language that is too broad invites drift. Language that is too narrow can restrict growth.

Clarity here protects future funding, partnerships, and strategic alignment.

---

## Practical U.S. Step: State Incorporation

When incorporating:

- Choose your state intentionally (often where you operate).
- Include required charitable purpose language.
- Add proper dissolution clauses.
- Align language with IRS 501(c)(3) expectations.

Poor drafting now can limit funding later.

---

# Layer 2: Governance Architecture

Bylaws define:

- Board size
- Officer roles
- Voting thresholds
- Term limits
- Removal procedures
- Conflict-of-interest standards

Boilerplate bylaws create predictable governance problems.

Bylaws must match:

- Organization size
- Growth trajectory
- Founder role
- Risk exposure

---

## The Bylaw Fragility Pattern

Organizations that omit term limits often experience:

- Board stagnation
- Declining engagement
- Founder entrenchment
- Political tension during transition

The issue is rarely personality.

It is structural negligence.

Bylaws define the structural rules governing your board. They answer: Who decides what? How long do people serve? What happens when someone doesn't perform?

Bylaws are not ceremonial. They are load-bearing. When governance questions arise — and they will — your bylaws are the document that prevents ambiguity.

Many founders file with boilerplate bylaws, then discover later that critical governance structures were never defined. Before filing, ensure your bylaws address eight essential elements: board size range, term limits, officer roles, removal process, quorum, committee authority, conflict of interest, and amendment process.

**→ Complete Tool 00 (Bylaw Essentials Checklist) in Appendix E before filing incorporation documents.**

---

## Layer 3: Authority Boundaries

Formation must clarify:

What does the board govern?
What does leadership execute?

Ambiguity breeds tension.

---

## The Authority Separation Principle™

Board governs.
Leadership executes.

When boards execute, they micromanage.

When executives govern, they consolidate power.

Both destabilize institutions.

Authority boundaries must be written — not assumed.

---

## Layer 4: Compliance Rhythm

Incorporation introduces recurring obligations:

- Annual state filings

- IRS Form 990 reporting
- Board meeting documentation
- Financial oversight reviews
- Conflict-of-interest disclosures

Reactive compliance creates risk.

Mature organizations establish rhythm:

- Calendarized reporting
- Quarterly governance reviews
- Annual board self-assessments

Predictability builds credibility.

---

## Reactive Compliance Collapse

Missed filings may seem minor.

But during due diligence, they signal instability.

Administrative negligence becomes reputational risk.

Formation without rhythm creates exposure.

---

## Layer 5: Documentation Infrastructure

From day one, document:

- Board minutes
- Policy adoptions
- Financial approvals
- Conflict disclosures
- Executive evaluations

Documentation is not bureaucracy.

It is protection.

Protection of:

- Leadership
- Board
- Mission
- Institutional memory

---

## The Practical Formation Sequence (U.S.)

To align structure with discipline:

1. Choose a name aligned with mission (avoid overly narrow branding).
2. Incorporate at the state level.
3. Obtain an EIN.
4. Draft customized bylaws.
5. Appoint governance-ready board members.
6. Apply for 501(c)(3) status only when governance and programs are clear.

Do not treat 501(c)(3) approval as proof of readiness.

It is permission to operate under scrutiny.

---

# Founder Action Blueprint

# The 30-Day Formation Readiness Review

Before filing:

**Week 1: Document Review**

Align Articles with mission clarity.

**Week 2: Governance Design**

Customize bylaws intentionally.

**Week 3: Authority Mapping**

Write clear board vs executive decision matrix.

**Week 4: Compliance Calendar**

Create an annual reporting calendar and a system for keeping records.

If this feels rushed, pause.

Formation without discipline creates future repair work.

---

# Decision Checklist

Before considering formation complete:

☐ Articles reflect mission specificity
☐ Bylaws are customized and understood
☐ Authority boundaries documented
☐ Compliance calendar established
☐ Conflict-of-interest policy active
☐ Documentation process standardized
☐ Board understands fiduciary responsibility

If incomplete, formation is cosmetic.

Cosmetic structure fails under pressure.

## From the Field: January 30, 2006

On January 30, 2006, Develop Africa was officially incorporated with the State of Tennessee as a nonprofit organization. IRS recognition as a 501(c)(3) followed — the Letter of Determination arrived April 26, 2006.

I remember the moment the paperwork was finalized with a feeling I did not expect: not celebration, but weight.

Because now it was real. Now there was a legal entity with my name attached to it. Now there were compliance obligations, a board to constitute, bylaws to follow, and a public accountability that hadn't existed the day before. The filing that felt like an ending — the finish line of a long process of deciding and preparing — was actually the beginning of something much harder.

Our founding board was composed of five people: my co-founder, a fellow Sierra Leonean, who played an essential role in the initial formation and launch of the organization; George, an international graduate student from Kenya studying in the United States at the time; Henry, an education professional; and Janet, a nonprofit professional with substantial experience who was based in Sierra Leone — and who had been my classmate at Fourah Bay College in Freetown. Janet brought expertise that none of the rest of us had: she held a master's degree in development and had worked with organizations including UNICEF and ActionAid. She understood the architecture of international development in ways that shaped how Develop Africa thought about its programs from the beginning. She served on the board for many years and was deeply committed to the mission. Janet passed away some years ago. Her contribution to this organization — and to the children it has served — deserves to be named. Five people who believed in the mission. Five people who were geographically scattered, personally stretched, and entirely new to formal nonprofit governance.people who were geographically scattered, personally stretched, and entirely new to formal nonprofit governance.

What we had was trust and commitment. What we did not yet have was governance discipline. Board meetings in those early years were conversations, not proceedings. Minutes were not consistently kept. George eventually returned to his home country and communication faded. Janet was in Sierra Leone, which made scheduling across time zones difficult before video conferencing was standard. Henry traveled frequently. The board existed, was legally compliant, and was composed of people of genuine integrity — but the rhythms of real institutional oversight took years to develop.

We were legally formed. We were not institutionally ready.

That gap — between legal existence and governance function — is where many organizations spend their first five to ten years. The paperwork says you are an institution. The behavior says you are still a movement. Crossing from one to the other requires intentional work that no filing with the state can substitute for.

Formation is where that work begins. Not where it ends.

---

## Founder Toolkit — A Mandatory Pause Before Filing

Legal formation is not the finish line. It is the starting threshold. Before any paperwork is filed, complete the Legal Formation Readiness Gate. This gate confirms your FRI score meets the threshold, your governance capacity is real, and you are not incorporating due to urgency or external pressure alone. Discipline postponed is instability guaranteed.

What January 30, 2006 taught me is that the paperwork is the easy part. Filing articles of incorporation, obtaining an EIN, drafting bylaws — these are administrative tasks with clear instructions and defined endpoints. A service provider can help you complete them in weeks.

What cannot be filed, purchased, or outsourced is governance readiness. The discipline to hold real board meetings. The commitment to keep minutes. The willingness to enforce conflict-of-interest policies with people you trust and care about. The capacity to receive financial oversight without becoming defensive. These are not legal requirements that arrive on the day of incorporation. They are practices that must be built deliberately, over time, by an organization that chooses to govern itself as seriously as it serves its mission.

If you are preparing to incorporate, the question is not whether you are ready to file. The question is whether you are ready to be accountable — to your board, to your donors, to your beneficiaries, and to the public trust that a 501(c)(3) designation carries with it. Filing is a day. Governance is the rest of your organizational life.

> **→ Appendix E — Legal Formation Readiness Gate**

Paperwork makes you legal.

Discipline makes you stable.

Formation is not a milestone.

It is a commitment to operate under public trust.

If you build it carefully, structure will protect your mission.

If you rush it, structure will expose your weaknesses.

*Legal formation creates the container. Governance fills it with accountability. Chapter 5 distinguishes between boards that merely exist and boards that actually govern — and provides a practical model for building a governing body capable of protecting mission, assets, and institutional longevity.*

# Chapter 5 — Build the Right Board (Not the Biggest Board)

## The Governance Function Model™

---

## Governance Is a Function, Not a Title

Many nonprofits recruit board members.

Few build governing boards.

There is a difference.

A board is not:

- A collection of impressive names
- A group of supportive friends
- A ceremonial oversight body
- A passive approval mechanism

A board is a governing authority.

Its function is to:

- Protect mission
- Protect assets
- Protect compliance
- Protect sustainability

When boards do not understand this function,
the organization becomes structurally exposed.

---

## The Governance Function Model™

A functioning board must fulfill four core roles:

1. Fiduciary Oversight
2. Strategic Direction
3. Executive Accountability
4. Institutional Protection

If even one role weakens, instability eventually surfaces.

---

# Visual Framework: The Governance Function Model™

INSTITUTIONAL PROTECTION

▲

EXECUTIVE ACCOUNTABILITY

▲

STRATEGIC DIRECTION

▲

FIDUCIARY OVERSIGHT

▲

MISSION & PUBLIC TRUST

Interpretation:

- Mission anchors governance.
- Fiduciary oversight protects resources.
- Strategic direction prevents drift.
- Executive accountability prevents power imbalance.
- Institutional protection ensures continuity.

Each layer depends on those beneath it. Neglect one and the weight redistributes — unevenly.

---

# 1. Fiduciary Oversight

Board members are legally responsible for financial stewardship.

This includes:

- Reviewing financial statements
- Understanding cash flow
- Approving budgets
- Ensuring internal controls exist
- Monitoring risk exposure

If the board does not understand finances,
oversight becomes symbolic.

Symbolic oversight collapses under scrutiny.

Action: Board reviews 90-day cash position quarterly.

---

## The Passive Approval Pattern

A board receives quarterly summaries.
No questions are asked.

Later, inconsistencies emerge during due diligence.

Board members say:

“We didn’t know.”

That statement does not reduce liability.

A board that asks no questions is not saving time. It is creating liability. Your silence will be read as approval — regardless of whether you understood what you approved.

---

## 2. Strategic Direction

Boards do not run operations.

But they must ensure:

- Mission alignment remains intact
- Program expansion is justified
- Growth matches capacity
- Strategy is periodically reviewed

Governance requires courage.

Avoiding strategic tension accelerates drift.

Action: Board annually reviews strategy against mission definition.

---

## 3. Executive Accountability

This is the most sensitive role.

Boards must:

- Set executive performance expectations
- Conduct annual evaluations
- Define authority boundaries
- Plan for succession

If the founder is never evaluated, governance is incomplete.

Healthy accountability protects both board and executive.

Action: Board conducts annual ED evaluation.

## From the Field: If You Build It

For the first two or three years of Develop Africa, I was the organization.

Not in spirit — in function. I made the decisions. The board, such as it was, affirmed them. Governance existed on paper. In practice, authority had never left my hands.

If you had been in the room at that time, you would have seen it clearly: a lot depends on Sylvester. Not because anyone designed it that way, but because no one had built anything different yet.

I knew it did not feel like governance. I felt the weight of it — the particular exhaustion of carrying an organization's decisions, relationships, and institutional memory alone. What I did not know was how to change it quickly. Board members who were committed were hard to find. The people I approached were cautious. Building something from zero is not attractive to most people. Everyone likes to join something that is already succeeding.

So I held onto a belief: if you build it, they will come. If the organization grew — if it became real, demonstrably useful, financially credible — better people would join. The board would strengthen. Governance would follow.

It was not entirely wrong. But it was naive about timing.

We started with four board members. Over the years, some left. Others joined. Slowly, the composition changed — from people who were willing to help to people who had something specific to contribute. People with industry experience. People who had served on other boards. People who asked harder questions and brought different skill sets to the table. The board that exists today — nine members — looks nothing like the board that affirmed my early decisions. Authority is distributed. Oversight is real.

Financial reporting includes variance analysis, year-to-date comparisons, and audited books reviewed by a CPA.

That transformation did not happen by accident. It happened because the organization became worth governing — and because I kept building long enough to find out.

Any founder in Stage 1 reading this should know: the weight is real. The isolation is real. The naivety is real. So is the possibility of what comes next, if you stay with it long enough.

But staying with it is not enough on its own. The belief that the organization would become worth governing if I built it long enough was only half right. What I did not understand in those early years is that governance capacity must be actively constructed — not passively attracted. Waiting for committed board members to appear is a strategy. But it is a slow one, and it leaves the organization exposed during the years it takes for the right people to arrive.

What accelerates the transition out of Stage 1 is not simply growth — it is the deliberate documentation of what the organization knows, does, and requires. When processes are written down, new board members can be onboarded. When financial systems produce clear reports, oversight becomes possible. When authority boundaries are defined, the founder can step back without the organization stalling. You cannot attract governance partners to a system that exists only in your head. You can attract them to a system that is visible, legible, and worth governing.

Build the organization. And build the systems that make it governable. Both are required. Only one of them was in the belief I carried through Stage 1.

## From the Field: The Room I Wasn't In

At some point in Develop Africa's governance maturation, the board introduced what is called an executive session — a meeting segment held without me present, during which board members review the executive director's performance, discuss organizational concerns, and exercise independent oversight.

I remember when this practice began. It was an adjustment for me. I had built this organization and knew it deeply. The idea that the board would deliberate about organizational matters without my input took some getting used to.

But I came to understand what executive sessions accomplish. They create space for the board to think independently, to ask questions, and to make decisions separate from the executive's perspective. That independence is essential to real governance.

Over time, I realized this was one of our strongest governance practices. It allowed the board to step fully into their role as decision-makers. It also meant I could trust the board's decisions because they were made without my influence shaping the conversation.

It's a structure that works best when the executive is willing to step back — not because their role is diminished, but because the board's ability to think independently makes the organization stronger.

Without it:

Power consolidates.
Blind spots expand.
Trust weakens.

If your board has never held an executive session — a meeting segment conducted without the executive director present — that is the practice to introduce next. It does not signal distrust. It signals maturity. A board that can only deliberate when the founder is in the room has not yet developed the independence governance requires.

The executive director's role in this is to step back willingly, to not ask what was discussed, and to trust that independent oversight makes the organization stronger — not because the board is adversarial, but because governance without independence is not governance. It is endorsement.

Introduce executive sessions before you need them. They are far easier to establish in a season of trust than to introduce in a season of tension.

---

# 4. Institutional Protection

Boards must think beyond the current year.

They protect:

- Reputation
- Legal standing
- Long-term solvency
- Leadership continuity
- Policy enforcement

Reactive boards operate under pressure.

Proactive boards operate with foresight.

Action: Board has discussed succession scenario.

## Board Composition Discipline

Early-stage boards should be:

Small.
Engaged.
Accountable.

Ideal size: **3–7 members**

→ Appendix E, Tool 08 — Board Orientation & Onboarding Checklist — ensures that every new board member understands mission, role, fiduciary responsibility, and behavioral expectations before their first vote.

More members does not equal stronger governance.

Clarity equals stronger governance.

Each member should contribute at least one capacity:

- Governance/legal insight

*If a candidate lacks financial literacy, provide training BEFORE seating them on the board.*

**CRITICAL:** *A board member who cannot read a balance sheet cannot fulfill fiduciary duty. Period. This is not elitist. It is responsible governance.*

- Financial literacy
- Fundraising or network leverage

Passive support is not capacity.

---

## The Relational Bias Risk

Boards composed solely of personal friends often avoid conflict.

Conflict avoidance leads to:

- Deferred financial oversight
- Unchallenged expansion
- Undefined executive evaluation

Harmony without accountability is fragility.

Respectful tension strengthens institutions.

---

## Governance Toolkit (Operational System)

Strong governance requires written records and rhythm.

At minimum, implement:

1. **Board Member Agreement**

**Visual Diagram: Board Governance Spectrum**

| **Ceremonial Board** | **Engaged Board** | **Governing Board** |
|---|---|---|
| Exists on paper | Attends meetings | Sets policy |
| Rubber-stamps | Asks questions | Reviews finances |
| No oversight | Ad hoc input | Evaluates ED |
| Founder decides everything | Founder leads with board | Shared authority with accountability |

Most early nonprofits begin CEREMONIAL.
Durability requires reaching GOVERNING.

   - Role clarity
   - Fiduciary duties
   - Attendance expectations
   - Fundraising participation standards

2. **Behavioral Expectations by Value**
   - Integrity
   - Accountability
   - Stewardship

- Respect

3. **Annual Executive Evaluation Process**
4. **Board Calendar**
    - Budget review
    - Strategy review
    - Compliance check

→ Appendix E, Tool 09 — Board Chair Facilitation Guide — equips the Board Chair to run structured, productive meetings that move from conversation to decision.

- Self-assessment

5. **Conflict of Interest Policy**

These documents convert goodwill into governance.

---

# Founder Action Blueprint

# The 60-Day Governance Stabilization Plan

Start here: schedule a board meeting within the next two weeks. Put this chapter's Decision Checklist on the agenda. Everything else in this plan follows from that conversation.

**Days 1–15: Role Clarity**

Draft board role descriptions and authority boundaries.

**Days 16–30: Board Agreement**

Require signed commitment outlining expectations.

**Days 31–45: Financial Literacy Check**

Ensure at least one member can interpret financial statements confidently.

**Days 46–60: Accountability Mechanism**

Establish executive evaluation process and term limits.

If this feels uncomfortable, that is a signal — not a reason to avoid it.

---

# Decision Checklist

Before declaring governance stable:

☐ Board size disciplined (3–7)
☐ Roles documented
☐ Authority boundaries defined
☐ Financial oversight active
☐ Executive evaluation formalized
☐ Term limits defined
☐ Meeting cadence consistent
☐ Conflict of interest policy enforced

If multiple boxes are unchecked:

Governance is symbolic.

Symbolic governance collapses under pressure.

---

## A Sobering Reality

A weak board drains more energy than a lack of funding.

Funding shortages are visible.

Governance weakness is subtle.

But governance weakness compounds faster.

---

> ### Founder Toolkit — Govern with Documents, Not Assumptions
>
> A board that has not signed a written agreement has not made a governance commitment. It has made a social one. Those two things are not the same under pressure.
>
> Use the Board Member Agreement to formalize expectations before a member is seated — not after a problem surfaces. Then run the Board Readiness

> Gate annually to confirm governance is functioning, not just existing.
> → **Appendix E, Tool 02 — Board Member Agreement | Board Readiness Gate**

The board you build early will shape the organization long after excitement fades.

Titles wear off.
Good intentions drift.
Structure remains.

Choose people willing to govern — not just agree.

*With governance structure in place, the next question is: what exactly will this organization do, and can it be clearly defined before seeking money to fund it? Chapter 6 establishes why program integrity must precede fundraising, and provides the framework for building programs that can withstand scrutiny at any stage.*

# Chapter 6 — Programs Before Fundraising

## From the Field: The Bedsheet Screen

From the Field: The Room Where It Began

*In December 2006, Develop Africa delivered its first program in Sierra Leone. The setting was a modest training room at iEARN Sierra Leone, located at the Stadium Hostel in Freetown. The walls were green. The desks were narrow. The monitors were bulky CRT screens from the early 2000s, their faint hum filling the room alongside the slow, deliberate clicks of new learners discovering a mouse for the first time.*

*There was no air-conditioning, no modern projector, and no Wi-Fi. A white bedsheet hung against the wall as an improvised projection screen. The projector sat balanced on a stack of books. When I adjusted the focus knob and watched a Microsoft Excel spreadsheet flicker onto the cloth, I did not know that this moment would shape the next two decades.*

*The program was made possible through two connections. Sylvanus Murray, Founder of YEDEM, had connected me with Andrew Benson Greene of iEARN Sierra Leone, who opened the facility for the collaboration. iEARN — the International Education and Resource Network — was not just a venue. It was a partner and a believer in the same conviction that had brought Develop Africa to Freetown: that technology could unlock futures, even here, even now.*

*For most of the students, it was their first time touching a computer. One young woman sat near the front, handling the mouse as though it might break in her hands. When she finally double-clicked and saw a window open on the screen, she gasped and whispered to her neighbor: "It worked." The entire row smiled with her. That small sound — surprise turning to delight — is the closest thing I have to a founding memory.*

*Power outages interrupted the lessons regularly. When the electricity cut out, we switched to theory — drawing icons on the whiteboard, explaining file structures in marker ink. When power returned, there were cheers, and students rushed back to their seats to practice what we had just discussed on paper. The curriculum that day was written on a flipchart: ICON. DESKTOP. TASKBAR. START MENU. FILE → EDIT → CURSOR. Simple words. But each one represented entry into a language that connected Freetown to the rest of the world.*

*That first program was not polished. It was resourceful. And resourcefulness, I learned in that green-walled room, is a renewable energy — one that powers progress even when electricity does not.*

*Years later, Andrew Benson Greene reflected on what began in that room:*

> *"Sylvester carried within him a rare combination of humility, conviction, and courage — a belief that educational technologies, when guided by compassion, could renew the minds and hopes of a generation. Those early Microsoft Office training sessions in Sierra Leone helped ignite a movement — one that continues today through digital literacy and computer empowerment programs across Africa."*

*— Andrew Benson Greene, Founder, iEARN Sierra Leone*

*The structural lesson from that first program is not about technology. It is about the willingness to begin before conditions are perfect. The projector was borrowed. The screen was a bedsheet. The curriculum was written in marker ink on a flipchart. None of that mattered. What mattered was that the room was full, the students were present, and the work began. Great movements rarely start with perfect conditions. They start with the courage to use what you have.*

The program existed before we had a grant to fund it. We designed the curriculum, identified participants, arranged the space, and started. Funding followed because the program was real, documented, and demonstrably useful.

That sequence — program first, funding second — became one of Develop Africa's foundational operating principles.

The Ebola crisis in 2014 tested that principle under pressure. When Ebola swept through Sierra Leone, we pivoted to hygiene kits and public health education. We responded to the need first. Funding followed. But this pivot also revealed the shadow side of that sequence: responding to need without asking whether you are equipped to meet it well. We knew how to run education programs. We did not have deep expertise in public health delivery or residential child care. The $30,000 grant that funded the Dream Again Home orphanage was real money for a real need — but the organizational capacity to manage a residential facility was not there.

The lesson from both experiences is the same: program integrity means knowing not only what you will do, but why you are the right organization to do it. Responsiveness is a value. So is honesty about your actual capabilities. The bedsheet screen worked because computer training was exactly what we were built to deliver.

Programs built on clarity survive scrutiny. Programs built on opportunity expose fragility.

## The Program Integrity Model™

# Funding Does Not Create Clarity

Funding clarifies nothing. It accelerates whatever structure already exists — or exposes the absence of it.

When funding is tight, founders are tempted to reverse the sequence:

Find the money first.
Figure out the program later.

That instinct is understandable.

It is also destabilizing.

Programs are not narratives to fit funding trends.
They are operational commitments.

Fundraising should amplify clarity — not compensate for its absence.

---

The Program Integrity Model

A structurally defensible program must answer four questions:

1. Who exactly does this serve?
2. What specifically happens?

3. What measurable change should occur?
4. What does it cost to deliver?

If any element remains vague, program architecture is incomplete.

---

Visual Framework: The Program Integrity Model

DEFINED COST STRUCTURE

▲

DEFINED CHANGE

▲

DEFINED INTERVENTION

▲

DEFINED POPULATION

COMPRESSED PROBLEM

Interpretation:

- The compressed problem anchors the program.
- Population defines scope.
- Intervention defines delivery.
- Change defines accountability.
- Cost defines sustainability.

Each element is load-bearing. Without all four, the program cannot defend itself under scrutiny.

---

# 1. Defined Population

"Communities" is not a population.
"People in need" is not a population.

Precision requires:

- Age range
- Geography
- Specific constraint
- Engagement timeframe

Programs without defined populations drift into general service.

General service dilutes measurable impact.

---

### The Undefined Beneficiary Pattern

A workforce initiative targets "young adults."

Participants range from 16–29.
Training varies.
Outcomes vary.

Reporting becomes inconsistent.

The issue is not effort.

It is population ambiguity.

---

## 2. Defined Intervention

A program must specify:

- Activities
- Frequency
- Duration
- Delivery method
- Responsible personnel

Clarity enables replication.
Replication enables measurement.
Measurement enables credibility.

---

## The Activity–Outcome Distinction

Many organizations confuse output with impact.

Output:
"We trained 200 participants."

Outcome:
"65% secured employment within 6 months."

Activity is motion.
Outcome is change.

The first is what you did. The second is what changed.
Narrative-driven fundraising survives short term.
Outcome-defined fundraising survives scrutiny.

---

## 3. Defined Change

Before fundraising, answer:

What will be measurably different within 12–36 months?

Examples:

- Literacy scores improve by X%.
- Employment increases within defined timeframe.
- Income stabilizes.
- School completion rates rise.

You are not promising transformation of the entire system.

You are promising defined change.

Ambition without measurement is aspiration.

---

## 4. Defined Cost Structure

Every program must answer:

- Cost per participant
- Total annual cost
- Major cost drivers
- Fixed vs variable expenses

Without cost clarity, fundraising goals become guesswork.

Guesswork erodes trust.

---

## The Funding Amplification Principle™

Funding amplifies whatever program architecture exists.

If architecture is disciplined,
funding accelerates impact.

If architecture is vague,
funding accelerates confusion.

Money does not solve structural ambiguity.

It intensifies it.

---

## Founder Insight

The strongest funding conversations I've experienced did not begin with large asks.

They began with clarity.

When we could say:

- This is the program.
- This is who it serves.
- This is what changes.
- This is what it costs.

Donors leaned in.

Confidence attracts funding.

Reversing the order creates dependency.

Dependency creates instability.

---

## The Program Defensibility Test™

Before seeking significant funding:

- Can you describe the intervention clearly?
- Can you quantify expected outcomes?
- Can you explain cost per participant?
- Can you articulate risk factors?
- Can your board defend the model?

If answers vary, pause.

Fundraising should follow clarity — not precede it.

---

## Founder Action Blueprint

## The 45-Day Program Stabilization Plan

**Days 1–10: Population Definition**

Document precise beneficiary profile.

**Days 11–20: Intervention Mapping**

Write step-by-step program delivery outline.

**Days 21–30: Outcome Definition**

Define 3–5 measurable indicators.

**Days 31–40: Cost Modeling**

Build basic program budget and cost-per-participant.

**Days 41–45: Board Review**

Stress-test program defensibility with governance.

If this sequence feels uncomfortable, that is a signal.

Clarity requires discipline.

---

# Decision Checklist

Before initiating a major fundraising campaign:

☐ Population clearly defined
☐ Activities documented
☐ Outcomes measurable
☐ Cost structure known
☐ Reporting capacity exists
☐ Board understands the model
☐ Program does not rely on founder overextension

If multiple boxes are unchecked:

Clarify first.
Fundraise second.

---

## Required Outputs

By the end of this chapter, you should have:

- Program one-pager (population, intervention, outcomes, cost)
- Annual program goals (3–5 measurable outcomes)
- Basic program budget
- Identified program owner

These documents do not just support fundraising.

They protect your organization from confusion, overreach, and burnout.

---

> ## Founder Toolkit — Define the Program Before Funding It
>
> This chapter has established that programs must be defined before they are fundraised. A program that

> cannot be described clearly cannot be funded responsibly — or evaluated honestly.
>
> The Program One-Pager forces that discipline. Complete it for every active program before approaching any funder.
>
> → **Appendix E, Tool 03 — Program One-Pager**

→ Appendix E, G5 — Program Readiness Gate

→ Appendix E, Tool 13 — Program Portfolio Dashboard

Funders do not fund organizations.

They fund programs they understand and trust.

Clarity is not a branding exercise.

It is structural leadership.

*Programs are defined. Now they need to be funded without compromising the clarity that makes them defensible. Chapter 7 addresses the financial infrastructure that supports trust — not because finances are complicated, but because financial opacity is one of the fastest ways to erode the confidence of donors, boards, and partners.*

# Chapter 7 — Financial Foundations

## The Financial Credibility Model™

---

## Financial Discipline Is Not About Perfection

It is about explainability.

Nonprofits do not lose donor trust because they make mistakes.

They lose trust because they cannot explain what happened.

Financial opacity erodes confidence faster than program failure.

Financial systems are not administrative burdens.

They are trust infrastructure.

---

Institutional financial stability requires five layers:

1. Separation
2. Documentation
3. Visibility
4. Forecasting
5. Oversight

If any layer weakens, credibility becomes fragile.

---

Visual Framework: The Financial Credibility Model

## Financial Credibility Model

Trust is built from the bottom up.

OVERSIGHT
▲
FORECASTING
▲
VISIBILITY
▲
DOCUMENTATION
▲
SEPARATION
▲
PUBLIC TRUST

Interpretation:

- Separation prevents exposure.
- Documentation enables explainability.
- Visibility supports fiduciary oversight.
- Forecasting prevents cash stress.
- Oversight protects institutional credibility.

Every layer depends on the one beneath it. Remove the written record, and oversight is blind. Remove separation, and accountability collapses.

---

# 1. Separation

From day one:

Personal funds and nonprofit funds must be separate.

No exceptions.
No informal reimbursements without documentation.
No blurred boundaries.

Even temporary blending creates narrative vulnerability.

Separation protects:

- The founder
- The board
- The organization

---

## The Early-Stage Mixing Pattern

A founder covers a vendor expense personally.
Reimbursement is informal.

Months later, records are unclear.

Nothing malicious occurred.

But ambiguity creates doubt.

Trust erodes because of confusion — not intent.

---

## 2. Documentation

Every financial transaction must have:

- Supporting documentation
- Clear categorization
- Approval trail

"If it's not recorded clearly, it didn't happen."

Documentation is institutional memory.

---

## The Explainability Rule™

At any moment, leadership should be able to answer:

- Where did this money come from?
- How was it allocated?
- Who approved it?
- What outcome did it support?

If those answers are not accessible within minutes, credibility risk increases.

---

## 3. Visibility

Financial statements must be:

- Clear
- Understandable
- Reviewed regularly

Boards must not simply receive financial reports.

They must understand them.

Fiduciary duty without financial literacy is symbolic.

---

### The Board Blind Spot Pattern

Quarterly reports are distributed.

No one asks questions.

Later, a grantor requests clarification.

Board members claim ignorance.

Ignorance does not reduce responsibility.

Visibility must be active — not passive.

---

## 4. Forecasting

Budgeting is static.

Cash flow is dynamic.

You can be "fully funded" on paper and still miss payroll.

A cash-flow forecast answers:

- When money arrives
- When expenses leave
- Where timing gaps exist

Even simple monthly forecasting prevents panic.

---

## The Timing Trap

A grant is approved — funds arrive 90 days later.

Meanwhile:

- Salaries are due
- Vendors expect payment
- Programs are running

The problem was not funding.

It was lack of cash visibility.

A simple monthly forecast answers: When does each funding source arrive? When must each expense be paid? Where are the gaps? Even three-month forecasting prevents crisis.

---

## 5. Oversight

Oversight includes:

- Board-level financial review
- Expense approval thresholds
- Dual authorization for major expenditures
- Conflict-of-interest enforcement
- Periodic independent review

Oversight protects leadership from suspicion.

It protects the board from negligence.

It protects the organization from structural risk.

---

## Required Early Systems (Non-Negotiables)

Before growth:

- Separate nonprofit bank account
- Bookkeeping system (QuickBooks, Wave, etc.)
- Monthly reconciliation process
- Defined expense approval structure
- Operating budget
- Program budgets
- Basic cash-flow forecast

These are not optional.

They are foundational controls.

---

# Founder Insight

Financial discipline is not about being perfect.

It is about being consistent.

The moment donors sense confusion around finances, confidence drops — even if impact is strong.

Clean systems reduce stress.

Clarity reduces fear.

Transparency multiplies trust.

## From the Field: Two Sets of Books

For several years, Develop Africa ran two financial systems simultaneously.

In the United States, we had QuickBooks. We could run variance reports, track spending by category, compare program costs to administrative overhead, and produce the financial statements our US board needed to govern effectively. The system was clean, legible, and auditable.

In Sierra Leone, Develop Africa Sierra Leone — our affiliated national organization, registered as a full NGO with the government, with operations formally launched in June 2015 through the Educational Lifeline for Pregnant Girls program — was running on Excel spreadsheets and Google Sheets.

This worked until it didn't.

The moment it stopped working was not dramatic. There was no crisis, no fraud, no missing money. There was simply a board conversation where someone asked a reasonable question: how much have we spent on programs versus administration in Sierra Leone this year? How does that compare to our budget?

We could not answer it cleanly. Not because the records were wrong. Because the structure of the records couldn't produce that kind of report. Excel captures transactions. It does not organize them into the categories, chart of accounts, and reporting layers that make financial oversight real.

It felt uncomfortable. We were running the finances honestly. We were recording income and expenditure. But we could not give the board what governance actually requires — not just records, but insight. The ability to compare actual spending to projected spending. The ability to see efficiency. The ability to answer the question.

That conversation made clear what needed to happen. We migrated DASL's financial records to QuickBooks. We built the same chart of accounts structure we used in the United States. The board treasurer in Tennessee got direct login access so he could run his own reports without going through me. When we later engaged an auditor to review the Sierra Leone books, the system was ready.

The lesson was not that Excel is wrong. It is that financial systems must match the complexity they are being asked to manage. A spreadsheet that captures transactions is a record. A system that organizes transactions into governable categories is infrastructure. They are not the same thing — and the difference becomes visible exactly when someone asks a question you cannot answer.

## From the Field: The SOP We Thought We Had

Writing the SOP is step one. What comes after is harder.

Develop Africa maintains beneficiary profile records in Airtable — a centralized database that tracks scholarship recipients, program participants, and their ongoing status. We have a written procedure: profiles should be reviewed and updated annually. The procedure exists. It is documented. It is not new.

This week I ran a spot check. I pulled a record at random and looked at the last update date. It was three years ago.

When I raised it, the response was reassuring: everything is current, the updates have been made. But the timestamp told a different story. The written procedure had not failed. The enforcement had.

This is the gap that no one talks about when they discuss SOPs: the distance between a documented process and a followed one. A procedure without an owner is a suggestion. A procedure without a review date is a historical document. And a procedure that staff can bypass by saying "it's fine" — without anyone checking — is not a system. It is paperwork.

The second lesson came from our scholarship program. We had a procedure for handling beneficiaries who dropped out of communication: a defined timeline, a set of contact attempts, a decision threshold. The procedure was sound on paper. What it did not account for was the reality of the communities we serve.

One girl became pregnant and chose not to tell us. She withdrew from contact — not because she had left the program, but because she was ashamed and afraid of what disclosure would mean. Another child was sent to a rural village to receive care from family during an illness. No phone. No way to reach us. The procedure said: if we cannot reach a beneficiary within a defined period, remove them from active status. The procedure was not wrong. It was incomplete.

Experience taught us what the procedure could not anticipate. We went back to the guidelines and built in exceptions: defined circumstances under which the timeline pauses, a process for family contact before any status change, and — where possible — an upfront conversation with beneficiaries and parents about what to do if communication breaks down.

SOPs are living documents. They require three things that writing them does not provide: an owner who is accountable for compliance, a review cycle that keeps them current, and a culture that treats deviation as information rather than inconvenience.

If no one owns the SOP, no one follows it. If it is never reviewed, it becomes a record of how things used to be done. And if the response to a gap is always "it's fine" — the system is not a system. It is a comfort.

Assign every SOP an owner. Set a review date. Check the timestamp.

## From the Field: The SOP We Wrote Because Someone Left

In the early years of Develop Africa, we had a part-time administrative assistant — I'll call her Grace — who handled donor acknowledgment for us out of our Tri-Cities office. She knew the process. She knew the tools. She knew which donors needed what kind of follow-up and when. When Grace left to pursue her studies, the process left with her.

What followed was an uncomfortable scramble. Donor acknowledgments through Network for Good — a platform we relied on for online giving — weren't being sent consistently. We were not meeting the IRS-required acknowledgment timelines for tax-deductible gifts. Donors who had given generously were receiving silence.

I sat down and wrote out the procedure from scratch. Step by step. Which donors triggered which acknowledgment type. What the timing requirements were. Where the templates lived. Who was responsible for execution and review. That document — a simple Google Doc — was last saved on February 24, 2012.

It was not a sophisticated system. But it was a documented one. And a documented system can be handed to someone new. A mental process cannot.

The lesson I carry from Grace's departure is not about her. It's about us. We had allowed a critical financial compliance procedure to exist entirely in one person's knowledge. When she left, the procedure left too. The SOP wasn't written because we planned well. It was written because we had to.

That's how most written processes actually get created — after something breaks. The goal is to write it before that happens.

Trust multiplies sustainability.

---

# Founder Action Blueprint

# The 60-Day Financial Stabilization Plan

Start here: if your nonprofit funds and personal funds share a bank account, open a dedicated nonprofit account this week. That single action closes the most common financial compliance gap in early-stage organizations.

**Days 1–10: Separation**

Open dedicated bank account and implement expense boundaries.

**Days 11–20: Bookkeeping Setup**

Establish chart of accounts and monthly reconciliation rhythm.

**Days 21–30: Budget Creation**

Build operating and program budgets.

**Days 31–45: Cash-Flow Forecast**

Project monthly inflows and outflows.

**Days 46–60: Oversight Integration**

Implement board financial review cadence and approval thresholds.

If any stage feels rushed, pause.

Financial fragility compounds silently.

---

## Decision Checklist

Before declaring financial foundations stable:

- ☐ Separate bank account established
- ☐ Documentation organized and accessible
- ☐ Chart of accounts structured
- ☐ Expense approval process documented
- ☐ Board reviews financials quarterly
- ☐ Cash-flow forecasting exists
- ☐ Conflict of interest policy active

If multiple boxes are unchecked:

Revenue growth will amplify risk — not stability.

---

> ## Founder Toolkit — Build the Financial Systems Now
>
> Financial credibility is built through daily discipline — not annual audits. Two tools from Appendix E support the work of this chapter directly.

> The Expense Approval SOP formalizes your approval thresholds, documentation requirements, and reimbursement process. The Operating Budget Template structures your revenue and expense planning with built-in board narrative prompts. Both should be adopted by the board — not simply used by staff.
>
> → **Appendix E, Tool 04 — Expense Approval & Documentation SOP | Tool 06 — Operating Budget Template**

Financial systems do not limit mission.

They protect it.

When finances are clear:

- Boards govern confidently
- Donors give with trust
- Leaders lead without fear
- Missions outlast individuals

That is not bureaucracy.

That is stewardship.

## Required Outputs

By the end of this chapter, you should have:

• A separate nonprofit bank account with no personal funds commingled

• A bookkeeping system (QuickBooks, Wave, or equivalent) actively in use

• An expense approval process with documented thresholds

• A basic cash-flow forecast covering the next 90 days

• At least one person on your board who reviews financial statements — not just receives them

These are not aspirational targets. They are the minimum financial infrastructure required before pursuing institutional funding. A funder who asks for financial documentation should never expose a gap that should have been closed before the conversation began.

*Financial systems are now in place. The question becomes: what funding strategies are appropriate for this stage of institutional development? Chapter 8 introduces a stage-aligned fundraising framework that ensures the pursuit of resources matches — rather than outpaces — organizational capacity.*

# Chapter 8 — Fundraising That Fits Your Stage

## The Stage-Aligned Fundraising Model™

---

## Fundraising Is Not a Shortcut

It is a structural consequence.

Many nonprofit conversations begin with:

"How do we raise more money?"

The more disciplined question is:

"Are we structurally ready for the money we are pursuing?"

Funding does not create maturity.
It magnifies whatever level of maturity already exists.

If systems are clear, funding accelerates impact.
If systems are weak, funding accelerates instability.

The Stage-Aligned Fundraising Model ensures that funding strategy matches institutional capacity.

---

The Stage-Aligned Fundraising Model

There are three general stages of fundraising maturity:

1. Foundation Stage
2. Stabilization Stage
3. Expansion Stage

Each stage has appropriate funding strategies.

Misalignment creates pressure.
Pressure exposes structural weakness.

---

Visual Framework: Stage-Aligned Fundraising Model

PROGRAM CLARITY
↓
FINANCIAL DISCIPLINE
↓
GOVERNANCE MATURITY
↓
INSTITUTIONAL STAGE

↓
APPROPRIATE FUNDING STRATEGY

Interpretation:

Clarity precedes revenue.
Discipline precedes scale.
Funding must match institutional stage.

---

## Stage 1: Foundation Stage

### Characteristics:

- Small team
- Founder-led operations
- Basic financial tracking
- Emerging governance discipline
- Pilot or single-program focus

### Appropriate Funding Strategies:

- Individual donors (founder-led)
- Peer-to-peer campaigns
- Small grants
- Monthly supporters

These streams require:

- Relationship-building
- Story clarity
- Basic reporting
- Light infrastructure

They do not require:

- Complex compliance
- Audit-level systems
- Multi-layer reporting teams

---

## Mini-Example: The Premature Institutional Grant

A startup nonprofit with minimal reporting systems applies for a six-figure foundation grant.

They win.

Within months:

- Reporting overwhelms staff
- Outcome tracking is insufficient
- Cash-flow timing causes stress
- Founder burnout increases

The grant didn't cause the instability.
Stage misalignment did.

Before applying for any grant above your current reporting capacity, ask three questions: Can we produce the outcome reports this funder requires with our current staff and systems? Can we manage the cash-flow timing if payment is delayed by sixty to ninety days? And can we absorb this program's demands without diverting the founder from governance? If any answer is uncertain, the right move is to build the capacity first — then pursue the funding. A grant won at the wrong stage is not a victory. It is a structural test your organization may not yet be ready to pass.

---

## Stage 2: Stabilization Stage

### Characteristics:

- Defined program model
- Clean bookkeeping
- Board oversight active
- Basic SOP documentation
- Clear outcome tracking

### Appropriate Funding Strategies:

- Mid-sized foundation grants
- Corporate partnerships
- Expanded individual giving
- Multi-year commitments

At this stage:
Systems can absorb complexity.

Expansion becomes possible — but controlled.

---

## Stage 3: Expansion Stage

### Characteristics:

- Mature governance
- Strong financial oversight or audit
- Measurable outcomes
- Documented systems
- Leadership depth beyond founder
- Revenue diversification

### Appropriate Funding Strategies:

- Large institutional grants
- Government contracts
- Major donor campaigns
- National corporate partnerships

At this stage, funding scales responsibly.

Before this stage, it creates pressure.

---

# The Funding Pressure Principle™

Large funding without systems creates:

- Compliance strain
- Staff burnout
- Governance exposure
- Reputation risk

Money does not strengthen weak architecture.
It amplifies it.

---

# The Donor Dependency Risk

An organization secures one donor covering 70% of budget.

Short-term relief increases.

But:

- Strategic direction shifts subtly
- Diversification declines
- Reporting becomes donor-centric

When the donor withdraws, crisis follows.

If any single funding source exceeds 30% of annual budget,

concentration risk is present. Plan diversification. If any source exceeds 50%, your strategy requires urgent attention.

Concentration without diversification creates fragility.

---

## Trust Compounds Faster Than Money

Fundraising is not primarily about asking.
It is about trust accumulation.

**Trust accumulates through:**

- **Consistent updates**
- **Honest reporting of challenges**
- **Clear financial explanations**
- **Outcome transparency**

Silence erodes trust faster than bad news.

Organizations that communicate only when they need money eventually lose relational capital.

---

## Fundraising Paths by Stage

Choose one path. Do it well. Then expand.

Early failure often happens because organizations try to do everything at once.

Clarity applies to fundraising architecture too.

---

# Path 1: Founder-Led Individual Giving

(Best for Foundation Stage)

What it looks like:

- Personal outreach to 20–50 contacts
- Modest repeatable asks ($25–$500)
- Clear single-program support
- Honest updates after gifts

Watch out for:

- Founder burnout
- No documentation of donors
- No transition plan

---

# Path 2: Peer-to-Peer Campaigns

(Foundation → Early Stabilization)

What it looks like:

- 30–45 day campaigns
- Supporters fundraising on your behalf
- Clear messaging templates
- One formal follow-up report

Watch out for:

- Overcomplicating structure
- Weak post-campaign communication

---

## Path 3: Small Institutional Grants

(Stabilization Stage)

What it looks like:

- Grants under $25,000–$50,000
- Clear program alignment
- Realistic reporting

Watch out for:

- Prestige chasing
- Admin underestimation

- Cash-flow timing gaps

---

## Path 4: Community-Based Fundraising

(Foundation or Stabilization)

Low-cost gatherings.
Clear purpose.
Clear documentation.

Watch out for:

- High-effort / low-return events
- Poor follow-up systems

---

## Path 5: Digital Giving

(After Communication Systems Exist)

Works best when:

- Programs are defined
- Communication cadence is consistent
- Impact reporting exists

Automation does not replace trust.

---

## The Fundraising Readiness Gate™

Before pursuing major funding:

☐ Program architecture is defined
☐ Financial systems are disciplined
☐ Governance oversight is active
☐ Reporting infrastructure exists
☐ Revenue diversification plan is forming
☐ Cash-flow forecasting supports growth

If multiple are weak, pause.

Fundraising should follow structural readiness — not precede it.

---

## The 12-Month Stage-Aligned Fundraising Planner

Each month, define:

- Primary fundraising focus (aligned with stage)
- 3–4 execution actions
- Communications sent

- Funds raised
- Lessons learned

This transforms fundraising from scrambling into discipline.

Consistency builds maturity.

---

## Value-Aligned Fundraising Decision Rules

If you value integrity:
→ Do not exaggerate outcomes to secure funding.

If you value accountability:
→ Match grant size to reporting capacity.

If you value stewardship:
→ Diversify revenue sources over time.

→ Appendix E, Tool 12 — Values-Based Board Decision Rules — extends this framework into a board-level instrument for evaluating any major organizational decision, not just fundraising.

If you value sustainability:
→ Build recurring donors before scaling institutional funding.

If you value transparency:
→ Communicate consistently — not only during campaigns.

---

## Hard Truth

Large funding does not stabilize weak systems.

It exposes them.

---

## Outputs (Required)

By the end of this chapter, you should have:

- A stage-defined fundraising strategy
- A 12-month action calendar
- A documented communication cadence
- A basic donor tracking system

Fundraising maturity is not about how many tactics you use.

## From the Field: You Are in Sales. Get Over It.

In the early years of Develop Africa, I wanted to play the background role. I am an introvert by nature. I was more comfortable building programs than talking about them. I believed, incorrectly, that good work would speak for itself.

A close friend named Phillip corrected me directly. “You are in sales,” he said. “Get over it.” That sentence has stayed with me for twenty years.

What Phillip understood is that donors do not give to organizations in the abstract. They give to founders they trust, stories they believe, and evidence they can see. The first $25 per month came from Erik, a supporter in Norway who found our website and decided the mission was worth a recurring PayPal commitment. That single donor, halfway around the world, proved something I had not yet understood: a clear web presence and an honest case for support could build trust with a stranger who had never met me.

The hardest fundraising period of Develop Africa’s history was not the early years of obscurity. It was COVID-19. Donations contracted sharply, and we had to scale back operations, delay staff payments, and ask our U.S. landlord for a temporary rent deferral. He agreed. We survived. But that season confirmed what Phillip had prepared me for: there is no stage at which fundraising becomes easy. There are only stages at which you become more disciplined.

It is about how responsibly you use the ones you choose.

---

Money sustains operations.
Trust sustains institutions.

When fundraising fits your stage:

- Growth becomes controlled
- Boards govern confidently
- Donors give with clarity
- Founders lead without panic

Scale is not the goal.

Alignment is.

What alignment actually requires is a check you should run before pursuing any funding source: does this funder's reporting requirement match our current capacity? Does their grant size match our stage? Does their program focus match our defined mission — or does it require us to stretch beyond what we have built to deliver well?

If the answer to any of those questions is uncertain, the fundraising conversation should come after you have resolved the uncertainty — not before. Funding that arrives before your systems can manage it does not accelerate growth. It accelerates exposure.

The right donor at the wrong stage creates as much structural risk as the wrong donor at any stage. Stage alignment is not a fundraising philosophy. It is a governance discipline.

## Visual Diagram: Stage-Aligned Fundraising Architecture™

INSTITUTIONAL MATURITY FLOW

┌──────────────────────────────────────┐
│ PROGRAM CLARITY │
│ (Defined population + outcomes) │
└──────────────────────────────────────┘

↓

┌──────────────────────────────────────┐
│ FINANCIAL DISCIPLINE │
│ (Separation + documentation + │
│ forecasting + oversight) │

↓

GOVERNANCE MATURITY
(Board oversight + executive
accountability + policy rhythm)

↓

INSTITUTIONAL STAGE
Foundation | Stabilization |
Expansion

↓

APPROPRIATE FUNDING STRATEGY

| Individuals → Grants → Major |
| Institutional Partnerships |

└──────────────────────────────────────

──┘

## Interpretation

Clarity builds discipline.
Discipline builds governability.
Governability determines stage.
Stage determines funding strategy.

Reverse the order — and pressure replaces stability.

When donors push for program expansion, the question isn't 'Does this align with our mission?' The question is: 'Can we deliver this completely, or should we say no?' Good intentions deserve respect. But respect means honesty: 'We appreciate your vision. We can only commit if we secure full funding before we approach a community. Are you able to do that? If not, can we direct your generosity toward strengthening our existing programs instead?' This is not unkind. It's responsible stewardship—of donor resources, of community trust, and of organizational integrity.

## The Setup

### The Computer Lab Story

Frequently, we receive requests from well-intentioned donors who have been contacted by someone in Africa—a friend, a contact, a partner—who describes a specific need. The request arrives with genuine urgency: "Can you send school supplies to this remote village?" or "Can you support a new computer lab here?" These moments feel like opportunity. Someone has identified a need. Someone is willing to fund a solution. The alignment feels natural. What's harder to see in that moment is the gap between donor intention and organizational capacity.

### Why This Happened

When those promises don't materialize, that hope doesn't quietly disappear. It transforms into disappointment—and obligation. The school community reached back to us asking why we couldn't complete what we'd started. They felt we'd made a commitment we couldn't keep. We hadn't legally committed more than we'd delivered. But we had created an expectation we couldn't fulfill.

Here's what we didn't anticipate: the community's expectations. When a donor visits in person and makes promises, those promises circulate. They become real in the minds of teachers and students. They create momentum. They create hope.

**The Hidden Cost**

What arrived was perhaps 30% of what he had committed to—some computers, some furniture, some structural improvements. Real contributions. But nowhere near the full scope of the computer lab he'd envisioned.

We did our diligence. We developed a Memorandum of Understanding. We verified his intentions. Based on his background and resources, we believed he was serious. Then, gradually, his availability shifted. We don't know why. Perhaps financial circumstances changed. Perhaps other responsibilities claimed his attention. Perhaps the initial enthusiasm faded as the reality of implementation set in. Whatever the reason, the support that had been promised didn't materialize as expected.

Several years ago, a kind-hearted gentleman in the United States approached us with a specific vision: he wanted to fund a computer lab in a remote village in Sierra Leone. He made a clear commitment—$20,000 to $25,000 to purchase equipment and establish the lab. He wasn't speculating. He visited the community in person, saw the site, met the school leadership, and seemed genuinely excited about the project.

**The Lesson: Mission Alignment vs. Donor Desire**

This wasn't a story of dishonesty or bad faith. The donor was genuinely well-intentioned. The problem was structural: we committed to a community based on a donor's promise without securing that funding upfront. An MOU isn't a guarantee. A visit and a verbal commitment aren't a guarantee. A donor's apparent financial capacity isn't a guarantee. What guarantees funding is: funding. In hand. Before you make promises to a community.

**The Principle**

Third, when we have a choice between expanding into new programs or deepening existing ones, we should choose depth. A partially-funded new initiative creates disappointment. A fully-resourced deepening of existing work creates sustainability.

Second, we should evaluate expansion requests against mission compression, not just mission alignment. A project can align with our mission and still violate our compressed problem. If we say we focus on literacy in Freetown, a computer lab in a remote village aligns with 'education' but violates the specificity that makes our work governable.

We learned three critical things. First, we should only expand into new programs when funding is secured upfront—not promised, not intended, but actually transferred. Either the check arrives before we approach the community, or we don't approach the community.

This experience forced us to ask a fundamental question: When a donor's desire expands our mission, how do we decide whether to say yes?

## Mini-Example: When Good Intentions Don't Match Capacity

## Founder Toolkit — Align Your Fundraising to Your Stage

The most common fundraising error is not a bad pitch or a weak relationship. It is pursuing the wrong type of funding at the wrong stage of institutional development. Two tools from Appendix E directly support the work of this chapter.

Tool 12 — Values-Based Board Decision Rules translates your organizational values into a decision framework your board can apply to any funding opportunity. Use it before saying yes to any grant or major gift that feels like a stretch.

The 12-Month Stage-Aligned Fundraising Planner in this chapter provides the monthly structure. Use it alongside the tool to build a fundraising calendar that matches where you are — not where you hope to be.

→ Appendix E, Tool 12 — Values-Based Board Decision Rules

*Fundraising is aligned to stage. Now the operational backbone must be documented so that delivery does not depend on the memory or presence of any single individual. Chapter 9 addresses the systems that ensure what you know doesn't leave when you do.*

# Chapter 9 — Systems, Documentation, and SOPs

## The Operational Continuity Model™

---

## Institutions Fail Quietly

They do not fail because people stop caring.

They fail because knowledge lives in memory instead of structure.

When processes exist only in someone's head, they disappear when that person leaves, burns out, or becomes overwhelmed.

Sustainability is not about effort.
It is about transferability.

Systems are not bureaucracy.
They are memory.

And memory is what allows institutions to survive change, growth, fatigue, and leadership transition.

---

The Operational Continuity Model

Operational stability requires five categories of documented systems:

1. Financial Procedures
2. Program Delivery Steps
3. Communication Workflows
4. Governance Processes
5. Onboarding & Training Protocols

If any of these are undocumented, institutional memory is fragile.

Fragility eventually becomes disruption.

---

Visual Framework: Operational Continuity Model

OPERATIONAL CONTINUITY

┌─────────────────────────────────────

─┐

│ FINANCIAL PROCEDURES │

│ (Approvals, recording, controls) │

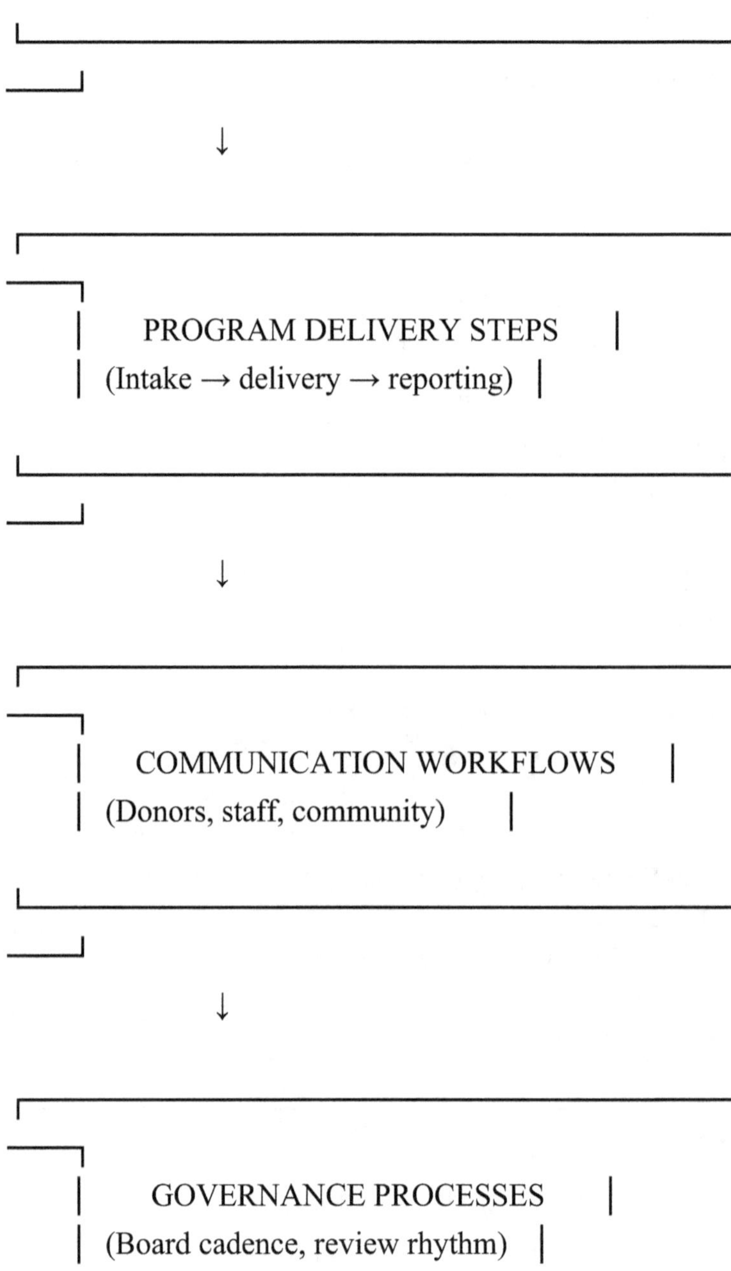
PROGRAM DELIVERY STEPS
(Intake → delivery → reporting)
COMMUNICATION WORKFLOWS
(Donors, staff, community)
GOVERNANCE PROCESSES
(Board cadence, review rhythm)

↓

│ ONBOARDING & TRAINING PROTOCOLS │
│ (Transferable knowledge) │

Interpretation:

Clarity becomes repeatability.
Repeatability becomes stability.
Stability becomes scalability.

---

# The Documentation Threshold™

**A process is not a system until:**

- **It is written**
- **It is accessible**
- **It is teachable**
- **It is repeatable**

Verbal explanation is not documentation.
Habit is not documentation.
Experience is not documentation.

Only structured, written process creates continuity.

---

## The Dependency Risk Pattern

When organizations rely on individuals instead of systems, three risks emerge:

1. Burnout Risk
   One person carries too much procedural memory.
2. Transition Risk
   Leadership change creates operational collapse.
3. Scaling Risk
   Expansion multiplies inconsistency.

Systems reduce all three risks simultaneously.

---

## Mini-Example: The Departure Shock

A program manager leaves unexpectedly.

Scheduling, partner coordination, and reporting processes were never written down.

You pause operations for weeks reconstructing memory.

The issue was not personnel.

It was undocumented dependence.

The question to ask before the next departure — not after — is this: if this person left tomorrow, what would stop? List every process they own that exists only in their knowledge. Each item on that list is a documentation priority. An SOP does not need to be sophisticated. It needs to be written, accessible, and understood by someone other than the person who wrote it. Dependence on individuals is inevitable at early stages. Remaining dependent is a choice.

---

## Core SOP Categories (Minimum Viable Architecture)

Every organization — regardless of size — should document at minimum:

---

## 1. Financial SOPs

• Expense approval process
• Budget development flow

• Payment processing steps
• Documentation retention

Example: Expense approval process with thresholds and sign-off.

Financial ambiguity destroys trust fastest. Document here first.

---

## 2. Program SOPs

• Participant intake
• Delivery steps
• Monitoring checkpoints
• Reporting cadence

Example: Participant intake → delivery → monitoring → reporting.

You cannot scale what you cannot describe.

---

## 3. Communication SOPs

- Donor update schedule
- Social media protocol
- Crisis communication pathway
- Escalation procedures

Example: Donor update schedule (quarterly), escalation pathway.

Communication failure creates invisible risk.

---

# 4. Governance SOPs

- Board meeting cadence
- Agenda structure
- Financial review sequence
- Executive evaluation process

Example: Board meeting calendar, financial review sequence.

Governance without documentation becomes symbolic.

---

# 5. Onboarding SOPs

• Staff orientation checklist
• Board onboarding packet
• Volunteer expectations
• Role clarity documents

Example: 30-day new staff checklist, role clarity document.

Transferability determines durability.

---

## The Replication Principle™

You cannot scale what you cannot describe.
You cannot describe what you have not documented.
And you cannot document what you have not first made repeatable.t you have not clarified.

Operational clarity precedes sustainable growth.

---

## Founder Reflection

For years, I was the system.

I answered questions.
Corrected mistakes.
Filled gaps.

It felt efficient.

It was not.

When we slowed down to document step by step, emergencies decreased.
Training accelerated.
Stress reduced.

Systems did not remove leadership.
They protected it.

## From the Field: The Staircase in Freetown

In 2009, I fell on a staircase in Sierra Leone.
It was not dramatic. I pulled a muscle in my back — badly enough that for the next two to three months, my physical mobility was seriously limited. I couldn't travel freely. I couldn't manage fieldwork the way I normally would. I couldn't be present in the way Develop Africa had come to depend on me being present.
Programs stalled.
Not catastrophically — but enough. There were decisions that didn't get made because I wasn't available to make them. There were coordination gaps because relationships and knowledge were concentrated in me. The organization

didn't collapse. But it paused in ways it shouldn't have needed to.

That fall was the first time I understood, viscerally, what "single point of failure" actually means. I had been reading the right management literature. I understood the concept theoretically. But lying on a bed in Freetown, unable to move easily, watching work stall because no one else knew how to proceed — that was different.

We were fragile not because our people were incompetent or uncommitted. It was fragile because too much lived in my head: relationships, process knowledge, decision logic, context that no one else had been given.

I did not immediately fix this. Change at that depth is slow. But I began paying attention differently. I started asking: if I weren't here, who would know what to do? And if the answer was unclear, that was the gap that needed to close.

A pulled muscle became the clearest lesson I ever received about documentation.

---

## The Simplicity Rule

SOPs do not need to be:

- 40-page manuals
- Complex diagrams
- Perfectly formatted binders

They need to be:

- Clear
- Step-by-step
- Updated periodically

A one-page checklist used consistently is stronger than a manual no one opens.

Consistency beats complexity.

---

## A Structural Reckoning

If a system only works when one person is present, it is not a system.

It is a risk.

---

## Value-Aligned Decision Rules

If you value accountability:
→ Document before delegating.

If you value sustainability:
→ Write processes before scaling.

If you value transparency:
→ Clarify workflow ownership.

If you value stewardship:
→ Protect institutional knowledge.

If you value integrity:
→ Ensure documented process matches actual behavior.

---

## Systems Readiness Checklist

Before declaring operational stability:

☐ Core financial processes are documented
☐ At least one full program SOP exists
☐ Reporting workflows are defined
☐ Governance processes are structured
☐ Onboarding materials exist
☐ Documentation is stored centrally
☐ SOP ownership is assigned
☐ Review cadence is established

If several are missing, growth will strain stability.

---

## Required Outputs

By the end of this chapter, you should have:

• At least 5 core SOPs
• A central documentation repository
• Named owners for each documented system
• A quarterly review rhythm

These do not need to be perfect.

They need to be real.

---

Systems do not replace people.

They protect them.

When knowledge is documented:

• Leaders breathe easier
• Teams work with confidence
• Transitions become smoother
• Organizations stop depending on heroics

Documentation is not administrative busywork.

It is how missions outlive individuals.

# Operational Continuity Model (Institutional Flow Format)

OPERATIONAL CONTINUITY ARCHITECTURE

┌─────────────────────────────────────────────────┐
│ FINANCIAL PROCEDURES │
│ Approvals | Recording | Controls | Audit │
└─────────────────────────────────────────────────┘

↓

┌─────────────────────────────────────────────────┐
│ PROGRAM DELIVERY SYSTEMS │
│ Intake → Delivery → Monitoring → Report │
└─────────────────────────────────────────────────┘

↓

┌─────────────────────────────────────────────────┐
│ COMMUNICATION WORKFLOWS │
│ Donor | Staff | Community | Escalation │
└─────────────────────────────────────────────────┘

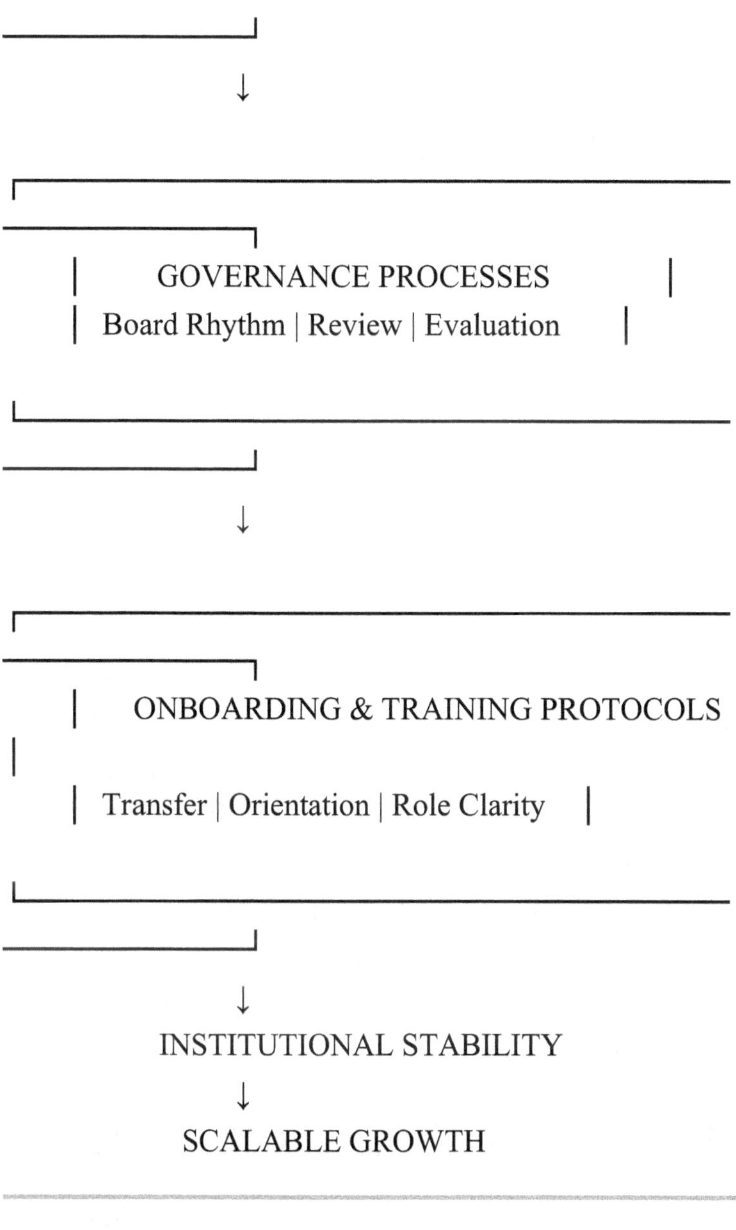


Continuity is layered.

Financial clarity protects trust.
Program clarity protects impact.
Communication clarity protects relationships.
Governance clarity protects authority.
Onboarding clarity protects memory.

When all five layers are documented, the organization becomes transferable — not personality-dependent.

Transferability creates durability.

## Part I: Structural Foundation

Chapters 1 through 9 have established the foundational sequence: from problem compression through operational continuity. The diagram below maps how each chapter builds on the previous one, showing the Mission-to-Systems architecture as a complete structural journey. Chapters 10 through 15 build on this foundation, addressing governance maturity, evidence discipline, scaling, founder sustainability, institutional case study, and the laws of durability.

# The Mission-to-Systems Flow Map

# From Idea to Institutional Stability

This visual shows how each chapter builds on the previous one.

---

# Visual Diagram: The Systemization Flow Map™

MISSION-TO-SYSTEMS™ FLOW

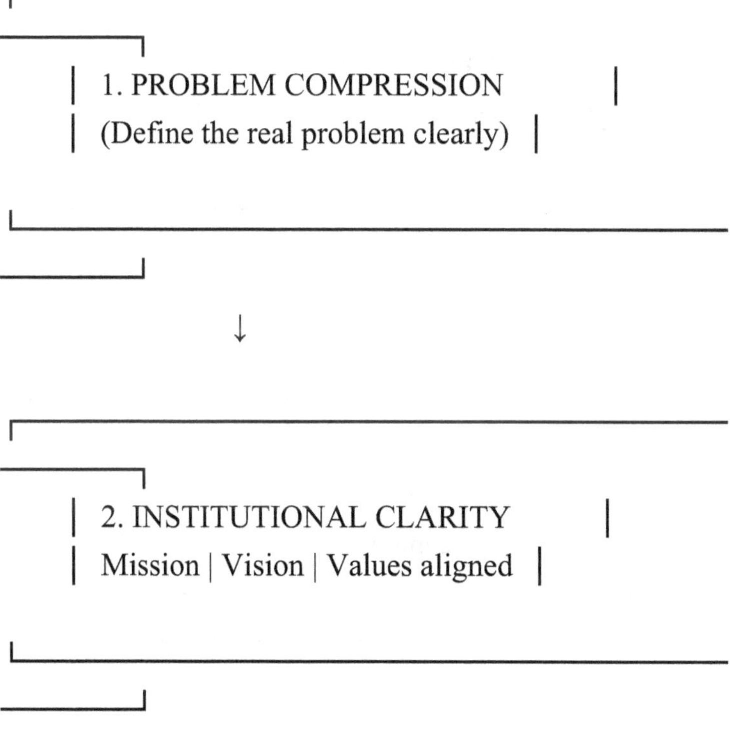

3. STRUCTURAL FIT
Choose the correct vehicle

↓

4. FORMATION DISCIPLINE
Legal + governance architecture

↓

5. GOVERNANCE FUNCTION
Board roles + accountability

↓

┌──────────────────────────────────────
──────┐
│ 6. PROGRAM INTEGRITY │
│ Defined population + outcomes │
└──────────────────────────────────────
──────┘
↓
┌──────────────────────────────────────
──────┐
│ 7. FINANCIAL CREDIBILITY │
│ Separation | documentation | trust │
└──────────────────────────────────────
──────┘
↓
┌──────────────────────────────────────
──────┐
│ 8. STAGE-ALIGNED FUNDRAISING │
│ Funding matches maturity │
└──────────────────────────────────────
──────┘
↓
┌──────────────────────────────────────

┐
| 9. OPERATIONAL CONTINUITY |
| Systems | SOPs | Transferability |

└──────────────────────────

┘

↓

INSTITUTIONAL STABILITY

↓

SCALABLE IMPACT

---

## How This Map Works Conceptually

This flow reinforces a powerful principle:

Clarity → Structure → Governance → Programs → Finance → Funding → Systems → Stability

Each chapter solves a structural risk:

## Chapter Risk Prevented

| Chapter | Risk Prevented |
|---|---|
| 1 | Misdiagnosed problem |
| 2 | Identity fragmentation |
| 3 | Structural misalignment |
| 4 | Legal fragility |

| Chapter | Risk Prevented |
|---|---|
| 5 | Governance weakness |
| 6 | Program confusion |
| 7 | Financial opacity |
| 8 | Funding pressure |
| 9 | Operational dependence |

This is not random advice.

It is institutional sequencing.

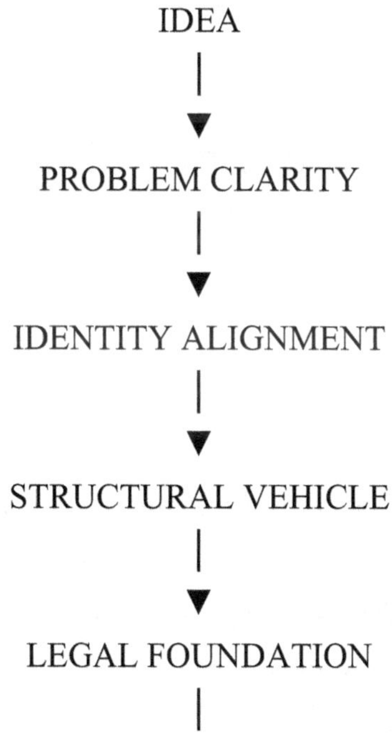

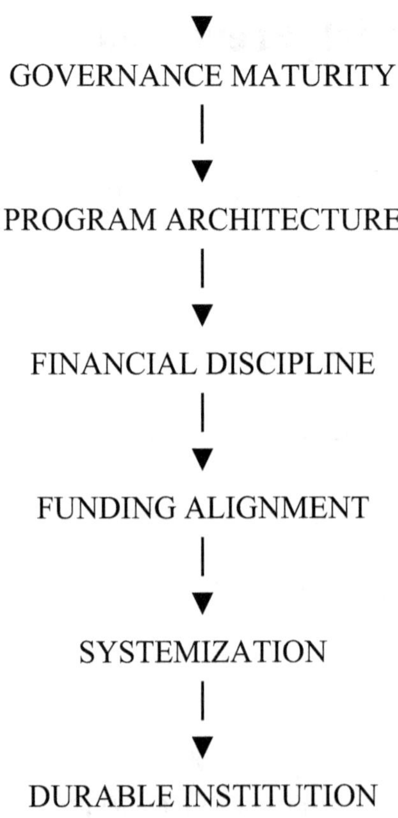


*Systems are documented. But paper alone does not ensure governance maturity. Chapter 10 examines how governance evolves across predictable stages — and why most nonprofit instability originates not from mission*

*failure, but from governance stagnation at the structural plateau.*

# Chapter 10 — Governance Maturity Doctrine™

The Governance Maturity Continuum

Almost every founder who reads this chapter will recognize their organization somewhere in the four stages. Most will be uncomfortable with the recognition. That discomfort is the beginning of governance work, not a sign that something has gone wrong.

---

## From the Field: December 5, 2015

I went back through the board minutes to find the moment I could point to.

The meeting was December 5, 2015. Four of us were present — one member joined by phone from outside the United States. We covered the Educational Lifeline Project, reviewed the health of the Dream Again Home, and then the treasurer gave his financial report.

What he said has stayed with me.

He reported that one of the areas we needed to improve was keeping our financial records updated. We had been lagging behind. We were working on finding someone to assist us.

That sentence — spoken plainly, in a board meeting, on the record — was a turning point. Not because the news was catastrophic. Because the board said it out loud.

By December 2015, Develop Africa had grown significantly. More income meant more transactions. More programs meant more complexity. The financial record-keeping that had been manageable between the treasurer and me was no longer manageable. We had not failed — but we had reached the edge of what volunteer effort and good intentions could sustain.

What I remember about that meeting is not the problem. It is the quality of the conversation. We were not defensive. We were not pretending. We looked at what we were doing, named what wasn't working, and made a decision: this is no longer something we can handle internally. We need to bring someone in who can dedicate fixed hours to this — someone accountable, someone consistent.

That is the difference between an organization that grows and one that stalls.

We had structure in place. We had governance on paper. We were raising money, securing grants, running programs. But we were not yet operationally disciplined. The December 2015 meeting was the moment we said that out loud — not to a funder, not in a report, but to ourselves, in the minutes, on record.

Governance maturity is not always a dramatic shift. Sometimes it is a treasurer's honest report in a small meeting, and a board willing to hear it.

## Governance Is Developmental

Governance does not appear fully formed.

It evolves.

Early-stage organizations operate under founder dominance.
Mature institutions distribute authority intentionally.

Between those two states lies the most dangerous phase of nonprofit life:

The Structural Plateau.

Understanding this progression is essential.

Governance evolves across four predictable stages:

1. Founder-Centric Governance
2. Shared but Informal Governance
3. Structured Governance
4. Institutional Governance

Each stage carries strengths.
Each stage carries risks.

Maturity requires deliberate movement — not accidental drift.

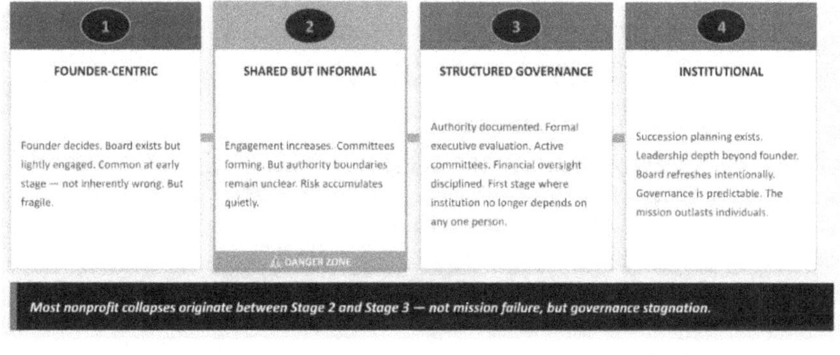


---

Visual Diagram: Governance Maturity Continuum

FOUNDER-CENTRIC
↓
SHARED BUT INFORMAL
↓
STRUCTURED GOVERNANCE

↓

INSTITUTIONAL GOVERNANCE

Alternate pyramid representation:

```
┌───────────────────────────────────┐
| INSTITUTIONAL GOVERNANCE |
| Transferable Authority   |
└───────────────────────────────────┘
      ▲
┌───────────────────────────────────┐
| STRUCTURED GOVERNANCE    |
| Defined Oversight        |
└───────────────────────────────────┘
      ▲
┌───────────────────────────────────┐
| SHARED BUT INFORMAL      |
| Growing but Loose        |
└───────────────────────────────────┘
      ▲
┌───────────────────────────────────┐
| FOUNDER-CENTRIC          |
| Personality Dependent    |
└───────────────────────────────────┘
```

---

## Stage 1: Founder-Centric Governance

### Characteristics:

- Founder makes most decisions
- Board exists but lightly engaged
- Financial oversight minimal but trusted
- Documentation limited
- Donor relationships personality-based

This stage is common and not inherently wrong.

But it is fragile.

If the founder steps away, instability follows.

---

## Stage 2: Shared but Informal Governance

### Characteristics:

- Board engagement increases
- Committees begin forming
- Financial review improves
- Strategic conversations expand

However:

- Authority boundaries unclear
- Policies loosely enforced
- Executive evaluation inconsistent
- Documentation incomplete

This stage feels mature.

It is not.

It is transitional.

Watch for the following:

- Board committees form but lack clear authority.
- Financial review improves but lacks teeth.
- Strategic conversations expand but lack decision discipline.
- You feel mature. But you are not.

---

## The Structural Plateau

*Figure: The Structural Plateau* — Governance Maturity Progression with Scoring Guide

The most dangerous phase lies between Stage 2 and Stage 3. Organizations do not fail at the Structural Plateau. They stall there. The discipline to move through it is what separates growing nonprofits from permanent startup-phase operations.

Revenue increases.
Staff grows.
Programs expand.
Compliance obligations rise.

But governance discipline does not deepen proportionally.

**Symptoms:**

- Board fatigue
- Founder defensiveness
- Inconsistent documentation
- Reactive crisis management
- Delayed compliance
- Informal decision-making

The organization looks stable externally.

Internally, strain accumulates.

Most nonprofit collapses originate here — not from mission failure, but governance stagnation.

---

## Mini-Example: The Plateau Pressure Pattern

A nonprofit grows from $150,000 to $1 million in three years.

Programs double.
Staff expands.
Board meetings remain informal.
Executive evaluation is absent.

When a major donor asks to see your governance records, gaps surface.

Growth exposed the plateau.

Governance did not keep pace.

The early warning sign of the Structural Plateau is not a crisis. It is a question you cannot answer. A funder asks for a governance document that does not exist. A board member raises an issue and there is no policy to reference. An audit surfaces a gap that everyone knew about but no one named. If you recognize your organization in this pattern, the work is not a governance redesign. It is three specific actions: formalize the board evaluation process, calendar compliance obligations, and activate at least one functioning committee. Movement through the plateau is incremental. But it requires deliberate movement — not more time at the same stage.

---

## Stage 3: Structured Governance

### Characteristics:

- Authority boundaries documented
- Formal executive evaluation process
- Core policies enforced

- Active board committees
- Financial oversight disciplined
- Reporting cadence predictable

Decision-making becomes distributed.

Founder authority becomes accountable.

Documentation becomes standard.

This stage requires intentional design.

It does not happen organically.

---

## Stage 4: Institutional Governance

### Characteristics:

- Succession planning exists
- Leadership depth beyond founder
- Board composition refreshes intentionally
- Risk management proactive
- Governance processes predictable
- Financial transparency proportionate to scale
- Portfolio review discipline

The institution no longer depends on personality.

It depends on structure.

Trust becomes scalable.

This is maturity.

---

## The Proportional Discipline Principle™

Governance maturity is not about size.

It is about discipline relative to complexity.

A $250,000 nonprofit requires governance clarity.

A $5 million nonprofit requires greater discipline — but the same principles.

Discipline scales with complexity.

It never disappears.

Chaos does not scale down gracefully.

---

## Authority Distribution Model™

Mature governance distributes authority across:

- Board (oversight)
- Executive (execution)
- Committees (focused supervision)
- Documented policies (decision guardrails)

Governance without clear authority boundaries creates the conditions for both conflict and concentration. The goal is neither centralized control nor diffuse confusion — it is documented distribution.
When authority is centralized, risk increases.
When authority is distributed, stability increases.

---

## Mini-Example: Founder Accountability Avoidance

A founder resists annual evaluation.

Board agrees “for flexibility.”

Years later, financial inconsistencies arise.

Because evaluation discipline never formed, correction becomes confrontational.

Early accountability prevents late crisis.

---

# Founder Dependency: The Silent Bottleneck

Founder dependency often begins as protection.

But when:

- Approvals require founder involvement,
- Donor communication depends on founder relationships,
- Strategy requires founder direction,
- Documentation lives in founder memory,

Governance maturity stalls.

Reducing founder centrality does not weaken mission.

It strengthens it.

---

# Governance Maturity Self-Assessment™

Answer candidly:

1. Could the organization operate for 60 days without the founder?
2. Is executive evaluation formalized annually?
3. Are authority boundaries documented?

4. Are financial reports actively reviewed by the board?
5. Are compliance deadlines calendarized?
6. Is succession discussed openly?
7. Are core SOPs consistently used?
8. Are donor communications predictable and scheduled?

If most answers are “No” → Founder-Centric
If many are “Partial” → Structurally Emerging
If most are “Yes” → Structured Governance
If consistently embedded → Institutional Governance

→ Appendix E, Tool 10 — Governance Maturity Scoring Worksheet — provides a structured scoring instrument to help you and your board assess current maturity across six governance domains and identify the specific gaps holding you at your current stage.

Honesty matters more than aspiration.

---

# Value-Aligned Governance Rules

If you value accountability:
→ Enforce annual executive evaluation.

If you value integrity:
→ Separate oversight from execution.

If you value sustainability:
→ Build leadership depth beyond founder.

If you value stewardship:
→ Treat governance as protective, not restrictive.

If you value transparency:
→ Document board deliberations consistently.

Values must be operationalized.

Otherwise, they remain aspirational.

---

# Governance Strengthening Roadmap (12–24 Months)

If you are Founder-Centric:
- Document authority boundaries
- Formalize board cadence
- Introduce financial review structure

If Structurally Emerging:
- Implement executive evaluation
- Activate committees
- Calendar compliance obligations

If Structured Governance:
• Develop succession logic
• Diversify board composition
• Conduct governance self-assessment annually

If Institutional:
• Stress-test systems
• Build leadership redundancy
• Prepare for founder transition

→ Appendix E, Tool 11 — Governance Maturity 12-Month Roadmap — translates your self-assessment score into a concrete month-by-month action plan. Download at www.missiontosystems.com/tools.

---

# Required Outputs

By the end of this chapter, you should be able to answer:

• Which of the four governance stages does your organization currently occupy — honestly, not aspirationally?

• What are the two or three specific governance gaps that are keeping you at this stage?

• What is the next concrete action that moves you toward the next stage?

Completing the Governance Maturity Self-Assessment (earlier in this chapter) is not optional. It is the output. An organization that cannot name its current stage cannot design a credible path to the next one. Governance clarity is not a report to produce. It is a decision to make.

## The Honest Assessment

Governance delayed becomes governance crisis.

The longer an organization remains on the Structural Plateau, the greater the correction required later.

---

Activity is not maturity.
Compliance is not maturity.
Growth is not maturity.

Maturity is disciplined structure aligned to mission.

Trust compounds when discipline is visible.

And when governance matures, the mission becomes durable.

*Governance is maturing. But governance without evidence is incomplete accountability. Chapter 11 introduces the discipline of impact integrity — distinguishing measurable change from mere activity, and establishing the measurement practices that protect both credibility and internal decision-making.*

# Chapter 11 — Evidence Discipline

## The Impact Integrity Model™

## From the Field: What We Reported vs. What Changed

For the first several years of Develop Africa's operation, our impact reporting answered one question: how many?

How many students received scholarships. How many participants completed computer training. How many families received supplies.

These are outputs. They are real and they matter. But they are not evidence of change. They are evidence of activity. And for a long time — longer than I am comfortable admitting — I did not distinguish clearly between the two.

What we were not measuring: whether the students who received scholarships actually stayed enrolled through graduation. Whether the computer training participants were using those skills for employment or income generation. Whether the families who received school supplies in September still had those children in school in June.

The shift came not from an external challenge but from looking honestly at our own data. Through internal review — team conversations, webinars on monitoring and evaluation, a growing commitment to continuous improvement — we started asking harder questions. What we found was uncomfortable: a significant number of scholarship students who made it through secondary school were failing their final English exams. Not because they lacked effort or intelligence, but because they had entered our program with weak English foundations, and we had never built in remedial support. We were measuring enrollment and completion. We were not measuring readiness.

That discovery changed how we designed programs. We began asking what additional support — after-school tutoring, language reinforcement, exam preparation — could address the specific bottleneck we had finally identified. Simple tracking systems followed: spreadsheets that monitored progress year over year, follow-up contacts at six-month intervals, pre- and post-assessments for training programs.

The measurement I wish I had started earlier was not complex. It was the question: compared to what we expected, what actually changed? That question, asked consistently, would have improved our programs faster — and would have protected more students from hitting an avoidable wall at the end of their secondary education.

Here is what evidence discipline looks like in practice, at the smallest scale: after identifying the English exam failure pattern, we added one column to our scholarship tracking spreadsheet. Exam results. Not just enrollment. Not just completion. Actual performance at the point of assessment. That single column changed how we designed the following year's program — remedial tutoring, earlier intervention, exam preparation support. One data point, asked consistently, shifted what we built.

You do not need a sophisticated monitoring and evaluation system to practice evidence discipline. You need one harder question asked at the right moment: did the change we intended actually happen? If the answer is unclear, that is where your program design needs to improve — not your headcount, not your geographic reach, not your fundraising.

Outputs tell funders what you did. Outcomes tell you whether it worked. The first earns the grant. The second earns the right to continue.

---

## Activity Is Not Impact

Nonprofits are naturally activity-rich.

Events.
Trainings.
Distributions.
Workshops.
Sessions.

Activity is visible.

Impact is measurable change.

Confusing the two is one of the most common institutional errors.

Organizations that mistake motion for progress become narrative-dependent.

Narrative-dependent institutions weaken under scrutiny.

This chapter establishes the discipline required to protect impact credibility.

---

## The Impact Integrity Model™

Evidence maturity requires four structural layers:

1. Output Clarity

2. Outcome Definition
3. Measurement Simplicity
4. Learning Feedback

Without these layers, credibility becomes fragile.

---

## Visual Diagram: Impact Integrity Model™

| 4. LEARNING FEEDBACK |
| Data informs refinement |

▲

| 3. MEASUREMENT SIMPLICITY |
| Consistent tracking |

▲

| 2. OUTCOME DEFINITION |
| What changed? |

▲

| 1. OUTPUT CLARITY |
| What happened? |
└───┘

Impact credibility is built from the bottom up.

---

# 1. Output Clarity

Outputs describe what you did.

Examples:

- 200 students trained
- 50 workshops delivered
- 1,000 meals distributed
- 300 families served

Outputs demonstrate activity volume.

They are necessary.

They are not proof of change.

---

# 2. Outcome Definition

Outcomes describe what changed.

Examples:

- 65% literacy improvement within 12 months
- 40% employment rate within 6 months
- 20% income increase among participants
- Reduced recidivism by measurable margin

Outcomes indicate movement toward resolving the problem.

Without defined outcomes, reporting becomes performative.

---

## Mini-Example: The Activity Illusion Pattern

A youth organization reports:

- 500 mentorship sessions
- 1,200 participants

When asked what changed, there is no follow-up data.

Initial applause fades.

Questions intensify.

The issue was not commitment.

It was outcome ambiguity.

---

## The Measurement Simplicity Rule™

Measurement does not require complex analytics.

It requires consistency.

Simple spreadsheets.
Basic surveys.
Pre- and post-assessments.
Periodic follow-up calls.

Complex evaluation models that are never implemented create illusion.

Simple systems consistently applied create credibility.

Clarity beats sophistication.

---

## 3. Learning Feedback

Measurement is not only for donors.

It is for internal refinement.

Evidence should answer:

• What worked?

- What did not?
- Where did results vary?
- What should adjust?

Measurement without learning is compliance. If you measure outcomes but don't use data to adjust programs, you are creating annual reports, not continuous improvement.

Measurement with learning is maturity.

---

## Mini-Example: The Data Avoidance Pattern

A nonprofit suspects outcomes are weaker than expected.

Instead of refining measurement, they reduce tracking.

Short-term reporting looks stronger.

Long-term credibility declines.

Avoiding data does not reduce risk.

It magnifies it.

---

## The Evidence Credibility Threshold™

To credibly claim impact, an organization must define:

- Baseline condition
- Intervention
- Expected change
- Measured difference

If any element is missing, claims weaken.

The goal is not perfection.

It is integrity.

---

## Transparency and Credibility

Transparency does not require perfect results.

It requires honest results.

Organizations that last are willing to tell the full story:

- Progress
- Setbacks

• Adjustments
• Lessons learned

Credibility compounds slowly.

It erodes quickly.

Silence erodes trust faster than weakness.

---

## Founder Reflection

Early-stage leaders often believe monitoring and evaluation is for large NGOs.

In reality, evidence discipline protects small organizations even more.

Tracking reduces self-deception.

It strengthens strategic confidence.

When you measure honestly, you lead honestly.

---

## The Self-Deception Risk

Without evidence discipline:

• Leaders assume effectiveness
• Boards assume success
• Donors assume impact

Assumptions are not sustainability.

Evidence protects integrity.

---

## Value-Aligned Evidence Rules

If you value accountability:
→ Define measurable outcomes before scaling.

If you value integrity:
→ Report strengths and weaknesses.

If you value transparency:
→ Explain how results were measured.

If you value sustainability:
→ Use data to refine programs.

If you value stewardship:
→ Avoid exaggerating impact claims.

---

# Decision Checklist: Impact Credibility

Before declaring impact credible:

☐ Outputs tracked consistently
☐ Outcomes clearly defined
☐ Baseline documented
☐ Measurement tools simple and repeatable
☐ Data informs program refinement
☐ Reports distinguish activity from change
☐ Board reviews outcome data annually

If several are inconsistent, impact credibility is fragile.

---

# Required Outputs

By the end of this chapter, you should have:

- Basic M&E Framework
- Quarterly Outcome Review Process
- Annual Impact Summary
- Donor Communication Calendar

---

# Annual Impact Summary Structure

Every year, your organization should produce:

1. Problem Definition (What problem are we addressing?)
2. Intervention Description (What did we do?)
3. Output Summary (What activity occurred?)
4. Outcome Results (What changed?)
5. Lessons Learned (What improved or struggled?)
6. Financial Summary (How resources were used)
7. Next-Year Adjustments

This document is not marketing.

It is institutional accountability.

---

## The Transparency Multiplier™

When evidence is disciplined:

• Funders trust faster
• Boards govern better
• Programs improve
• Strategy sharpens
• Leaders operate with confidence

Trust multiplies through visible discipline.

---

Governance protects the institution.

Systems protect operations.

Financial clarity protects credibility.

Evidence discipline protects mission truth.

Activity is not maturity.

Growth is not maturity.

Narrative is not maturity.

Maturity is disciplined structure aligned to measurable change.

When impact can be explained clearly and honestly,
the mission becomes durable.

*Evidence discipline is now established. The organization is being measured honestly. The next temptation — and the next risk — is growth. Chapter 12 examines the structural conditions required before expansion begins, and why scaling without proportional institutional strength always produces the same outcome: fracture.*

# Chapter 12 — Scaling Without Breaking

## Growth Is Not the Goal

Durability is.

In the nonprofit world, growth is often treated as validation.

More revenue. More programs. More staff. More locations.

Expansion is assumed to equal progress.

But growth is not inherently virtuous.

## Growth magnifies what already exists.

If structure is strong, growth increases impact. If structure is weak, growth increases strain.

The question is not whether an organization can grow.

The question is whether it can grow without breaking.

---

## The Structural Scaling Model™

Before scale, four capacities must deepen proportionally:

1. **Governance Capacity**
2. **Operational Capacity**
3. **Financial Capacity**
4. **Leadership Capacity**

If scale occurs without proportional strengthening in these domains, fracture follows.

Scaling is not multiplication of activity.

It is multiplication of complexity.

---

## The Complexity Threshold Principle™

Every growth milestone introduces new layers of complexity.

## At $250,000 annually:

- Informal systems can survive.
- Direct oversight is manageable.
- Founder coordination is efficient.

## At $1 million:

- Reporting requirements increase.

- Staff coordination multiplies.
- Financial scrutiny deepens.
- Decision bottlenecks surface.

## At $5 million:

- Governance expectations rise sharply.
- Compliance exposure expands.
- Reputation risk increases.
- Leadership depth becomes non-negotiable.

Revenue does not scale linearly with complexity.

Complexity accelerates faster than revenue.

Organizations that fail to anticipate this threshold experience strain that feels sudden — but was structurally predictable.

---

# 1. Governance Capacity

As revenue increases:

- Regulatory scrutiny intensifies.
- Stakeholder expectations expand.
- Board responsibility deepens.

- Risk exposure multiplies.

The governance structure that functioned at startup will not function at scale.

## Questions to examine before expansion:

- Are board roles clearly defined?
- Are financial reports actively reviewed?
- Are committees functioning with clarity?
- Is executive performance formally evaluated?
- Is risk oversight proactive rather than reactive?

## Scaling without governance deepening creates:

- Authority confusion
- Compliance exposure
- Board fatigue
- Founder defensiveness

Governance must evolve before scale, not after strain arrives.

## Mini-Example: The Growth–Governance Gap

A nonprofit doubles its revenue in two years.

Programs expand. Staff increases.

But board composition remains unchanged. Meeting cadence remains informal. Committee structure remains undefined.

When a funder requests governance documentation, gaps surface.

The program did not fail because it grew.

It strained because governance maturity did not deepen proportionally.

Growth revealed the lag.

The question that closes this gap is not "how do we grow faster?" It is "has our governance capacity grown proportionally with our programs?" Before the next expansion — new program, new geography, new staff — run this check: does our board composition match the complexity we are about to take on? Are our financial systems capable of managing the reporting this growth will require? Are our SOPs documented well enough that new staff can be onboarded without the founder's direct involvement? If any answer is no, that is where the next investment goes. Not into the expansion. Into the infrastructure that makes the expansion survivable.

## 2. Operational Capacity

Operational systems are stress-tested under scale.

Expansion multiplies:

- Staff communication complexity
- Cross-team coordination
- Documentation needs
- Reporting volume
- Partner relationships

If SOPs were loosely followed at small scale, inconsistency becomes systemic at larger scale.

You cannot scale improvisation.

## Operational maturity requires:

- Documented workflows
- Clear approval pathways
- Defined reporting cadences
- Standardized onboarding
- Clear escalation channels

Expansion without documented processes increases confusion exponentially.

Consistency must precede replication.

## The Replication Rule™

### If you cannot describe a process clearly, you cannot replicate it reliably.

If replication is inconsistent, outcomes will vary.

If outcomes vary unpredictably, credibility erodes.

Operational clarity is not bureaucracy.

It is scalability insurance.

---

## 3. Financial Capacity

Revenue growth often feels stabilizing.

But financial strain increases under scale:

- Payroll commitments expand.
- Fixed costs rise.
- Vendor obligations deepen.
- Cash flow timing becomes critical.
- Audit expectations increase.

Organizations often celebrate revenue growth while ignoring structural exposure.

## The Revenue Spike Risk

A nonprofit secures a large multi-year grant.

Hiring accelerates. Programs expand. Fixed costs increase.

Two years later, renewal fails.

Revenue drops sharply.

Layoffs follow.

Morale declines.

Reputation absorbs damage.

The issue was not funding.

It was over-scaling fixed costs without diversification.

## Scaling must include:

- Cash flow forecasting
- Scenario modeling
- Revenue diversification strategy
- Conservative fixed-cost growth
- Clear reserves policy

Revenue growth without diversification creates concentration risk.

Diversification protects stability.

---

# 4. Leadership Capacity

Founder-led organizations often reach a ceiling.

At scale, leadership must shift from operator to architect.

That transition includes:

- Delegating execution
- Developing middle management
- Accepting oversight structures
- Distributing authority
- Building succession logic

Founder control that was efficient early becomes restrictive later.

# Scaling programs without scaling leadership capacity creates:

- Decision bottlenecks
- Delayed approvals

- Overextension
- Founder burnout
- Staff dependency

Leadership must evolve alongside size.

## The Leadership Bandwidth Limit

Many organizations plateau not because funding is insufficient — but because leadership bandwidth is exhausted.

Growth slows not from scarcity, but from concentration.

## Scaling leadership precedes scaling geography.

---

## From the Field: The Microfinance Lesson

As our scholarship program grew, we received requests from beneficiary families asking if we could provide microfinance loans to help them start or expand small businesses. The families understood our mission. They had benefited from our support. The request made sense.

On paper, it sounded promising. In practice, it taught us something uncomfortable about scaling.

What it taught us was this: mission adjacency is not the same as mission alignment.

The families who requested the loans were not wrong to ask. They had benefited from our work. They trusted us. And the request felt like a natural extension of what Develop Africa had already built — relationships, credibility, and resources directed at the same community. That logic is exactly how mission creep begins. Not with a bad idea, but with a good relationship and an understandable request.

Running a microfinance program requires a specific and separate set of capacities: loan underwriting, repayment tracking, default management, financial counseling, and the institutional will to enforce consequences when payments stop. These are not harder or easier than running an education program. They are different. And Develop Africa had spent years building capacity for one thing, not the other.

When the program strained — when repayment rates declined, defaults accumulated, and the financial and leadership capacity to manage it collapsed — the root cause was not the families who defaulted. It was us. We had entered a field we were not built for, with the resources of an organization built for something else.

The question every founder must ask before expanding is not “Does this serve our community?” It is “Are we the right organization to serve this need, with this capacity, at this stage?” Those are different questions. The first is about compassion. The second is about governance. Both matter. But only the second protects you from a well-intentioned failure.

Chapter 12 examines the four capacities — Financial, Leadership, Operational, and Program — and how the failure of any one creates a cascade that damages the others.

## The Structure That Worked

We began with thoughtful design. A board member took governance responsibility for the program. We established a tiered approach: initial business training for all loan recipients, monthly peer-to-peer sessions where borrowers could share challenges and successes, clear documentation of loan terms and repayment schedules, and regular monitoring visits.

The early results were encouraging. Beneficiaries were grateful and enthusiastic. When I visited several recipients during one of my trips to Sierra Leone, I saw genuine business growth — small ventures expanding, families investing in their children's futures, hope taking tangible form. The program was working.

## The Degradation

What I did not anticipate was what would happen as the program scaled.

Over the next two to three years, we gradually and unintentionally abandoned every element that had made it work.

The board member's time was needed elsewhere, so governance responsibility became diffuse. Training sessions, initially rigorous, became inconsistent and eventually optional — we assumed that early cohorts understood the principles and could teach later ones. Peer sessions, which had created accountability and mutual support, simply stopped. And expectations for reporting — what updates we wanted from borrowers, what communication we expected — became vague. We had never formally documented these expectations, so they existed mainly as an internal feeling about how things "should" work.

As structure degraded, so did outcomes. Over four years, repayment rates declined steadily. Borrowers became less willing to provide updates on their businesses. Payment schedules became irregular. Defaults accumulated.

## The Difficult Truth

When defaults began, I had to stop and ask an uncomfortable question: What did we do wrong?

The answer was not that beneficiaries were dishonest or uncommitted. It was that we had systematically removed the structure that allowed the program to function.

But there was another layer to this failure — one that forced an even harder reckoning.

As repayment problems mounted, we discovered that the circumstances facing our beneficiaries were far more complex than our loan framework could accommodate. One family faced a medical crisis and made the choice to use the loan money for hospitalization rather than business investment. Another experienced a market collapse that made business expansion impossible. A third simply faced the mathematics of survival: with minimal income, the choice between feeding their family and maintaining a loan repayment schedule was no choice at all.

We could have blamed the borrowers for defaulting. Instead, we had to confront the reality that our system was designed for ideal circumstances — people with stable income, predictable family situations, and the luxury of prioritizing debt repayment over survival.

Our microfinance program failed not because the concept was flawed, but because we scaled it without the supporting structure, and because even with structure, we had designed it without sufficient flexibility for the realities of people's lives.

We had created a system that prioritized our reporting metrics — repayment rates, successful loan closures, portfolio performance — over the actual human outcomes we claimed to value.

**The honest question became: What does success mean in this context?** Is it a clean financial record? Or is it families lifted out of poverty, even if the path to that outcome doesn't match our original loan terms?

For some borrowers, the money had genuinely helped — had enabled them to weather a crisis, invest in their children's education, or stabilize their families. But they couldn't repay the loan because the money had been used for survival, not business growth. By our original metrics, these were failures. By any honest measure of impact, they were successes.

## What We Changed

We made several decisions that reflect what we learned:

First, we paused the program rather than continuing to collect on defaulted loans. We wanted to address the underlying structural problems before expanding further.

Second, we forgave certain loans where it became clear the money had genuinely uplifted families but couldn't be repaid within a reasonable timeline.

Third, we began redesigning around a different model — moving from strictly repayment-based loans to a hybrid approach that includes grants for families in genuine crisis.

Fourth, and perhaps most importantly, we committed to rebuilding structure before scaling again. If we return to microfinance, we will do so with renewed commitment to the training, peer accountability, clear expectations, and regular monitoring that made the early program work.

## The Deeper Lesson

This experience crystallized something I was learning across all of our programs: **Structure doesn't mature past the need for structure. It either scales proportionally with the program, or it degrades.**

When a program feels established, the instinct is to reduce oversight — to assume it can run more efficiently with less supervision. The opposite is true. As a program scales, structure must scale with it. The training becomes more important, not less. The accountability mechanisms become more critical, not less. The clarity about expectations becomes more necessary, not less.

The microfinance program taught us that scaling a **degraded system spreads degradation faster.**

But it also taught us something else: that metrics alone can hide what's actually happening. A 100% repayment rate would have looked like success. A 50% repayment rate looked like failure. But neither number told us what we actually needed to know — whether we were genuinely uplifting the families we served, or simply imposing a structure that worked for our reporting requirements, not their circumstances.

True impact measurement requires asking: Did the resources we provided actually improve this family's situation? If the answer is yes, even if the loan couldn't be repaid, we should be honest about that. We should count it as success and figure out how to report it accurately, rather than dismissing it as a failed loan.

---

## The Four Capacities: How the Microfinance Program Failed

Each of the three structural collapses maps directly to a capacity failure.

## Mapping the Failures to Your Four Capacities

| Capacity | What Should Happen | In the Microfinance Program | What Failed |
|---|---|---|---|
| **Governance Capacity** | Board oversight remains consistent; clear responsibility assigned | Board member withdrew; governance became diffuse | No one was ultimately responsible for program quality or oversight |
| **Operational Capacity** | Processes become more documented and rigorous as you scale | Training stopped (Failure #1); peer sessions ended (Failure #2); expectations unclear (Failure #3) | No two loan cycles operated the same way; inconsistency became systemic |
| **Financial Capacity** | Project default rates; build reserves; understand risk | We didn't anticipate or prepare for increasing defaults | Defaults created a crisis rather than an anticipated risk we had planned for |

| Capacity | What Should Happen | In the Microfinance Program | What Failed |
|---|---|---|---|
| **Leadership Capacity** | Responsibility is clearly distributed as the program grows | Program responsibility was never redistributed to anyone; it simply faded | Nobody owned the program; nobody was accountable for its decline |

# The Pattern

Notice what happened: **All three failures cascaded across all four capacities.**

The microfinance program didn't fail because we scaled carelessly. It failed because we abandoned the structure that had made it work — and we did so across multiple capacities simultaneously.

**Each capacity is connected.** When one degrades, others follow:

- No clear Governance Capacity → No accountability (Leadership Capacity)
- No accountability → Training becomes optional (Operational Capacity)
- Training stops → Borrowers unprepared (Operational Capacity)

- Unprepared borrowers → Increasing defaults (Financial Capacity) → Program crisis (all capacities)

---

# The Expansion vs. Consolidation Cycle™

Mature institutions alternate intentionally between two phases:

**Expansion phases:** Add programs, staff, or geography

- 12–18 months of growth
- New initiatives launch
- Complexity increases

**Consolidation phases:** Strengthen governance, refine SOPs, deepen financial oversight

- 6–12 months of stabilization
- No new programs initiated
- Focus shifts inward
- Systems strengthen

# The Rhythm

Organizations that expand continuously without consolidation accumulate fragility.

Consolidation is not stagnation.

It is reinforcement.

During consolidation phases, institutions:

- Audit governance structures
- Refine SOPs and documentation
- Review financial forecasting
- Strengthen board engagement
- Clarify delegation
- Improve reporting systems
- Build reserves

Only after consolidation should expansion resume.

## Danger Sign: Continuous Expansion Without Consolidation

The microfinance program shows what happens: continuous expansion (new borrowers, growing loan volume) without consolidation (no time to formalize training, no refining of peer accountability, no clarifying of expectations).

The program grew, but it was never consolidated.

By the time defaults arrived, there was no time to pause and strengthen — the program had already begun to fail.

---

## The Scaling Readiness Test™

Before expanding programs, geography, or staffing, ask:

## Governance Capacity:

- Is governance stable and active?
- Are board roles clearly defined?
- Is executive performance evaluated?

## Operational Capacity:

- Are SOPs documented and used consistently?
- Could new staff learn the processes from documentation?
- Is quality control systematic?

## Financial Capacity:

- Is cash flow predictable?
- Is revenue diversified?
- Have default/risk scenarios been modeled?

## Leadership Capacity:

- Is reporting disciplined?
- Is leadership distributed?
- Has a consolidation phase occurred recently?

If multiple answers are unclear, scale cautiously.

Stress becomes burnout. Burnout becomes instability. Instability damages reputation.

## Growth delayed is safer than growth reversed.

---

## Visual Framework: The Scaling Readiness Matrix™

| **Funding** | **Systems Weak** | **Systems Strong** |
|---|---|---|
| **Funding Available** | **High Risk:** Growth exposes fragility fast | **Scale-Ready:** Resources align with capacity |
| **Funding Limited** | **Stable Danger:** Systems weak, no pressure yet | **Build Phase:** Strengthen before seeking funding |

+-----------+--------------------+-------------------+

**RULE:** Strong systems + funding = scale.

**RULE:** Weak systems + any funding = risk.

---

## The Unvarnished Truth

## Scaling a broken system only spreads the damage faster.

Growth is visible.

Durability is structural.

Institutions that endure do not scale impulsively.

They scale deliberately.

They reinforce before they expand.

They consolidate before they multiply.

Mission initiates growth.

Structure determines whether it survives.

---

## Founder Reflection

Growth feels validating.

It signals momentum. It signals relevance.

But expansion without structural readiness creates silent fragility.

The discipline to delay scale is a mark of institutional maturity.

Saying "not yet" is more responsible than saying "yes."

Scaling is not ambition alone.

It is ambition disciplined by structure.

---

## Founder Toolkit — Scale With Structure, Not Momentum

Before initiating any significant expansion — new program, new geography, new staff — two tools from Appendix E provide the structural check your board should complete.

Tool 10 — Governance Maturity Scoring Worksheet will tell you whether your governance infrastructure is ready to absorb the complexity growth brings. If the score reveals Stage 1 or Stage 2 governance, that is the work before the expansion — not after.

Tool 13 — Program Portfolio Dashboard evaluates your existing programs against capacity, funding, and mission alignment before you add another one.

→ Appendix E, Tool 10 — Governance Maturity Scoring Worksheet

→ Appendix E, Tool 13 — Program Portfolio Dashboard

Scaling strategy is defined. But no scaling plan survives founder dependency.

Chapter 13 addresses the most personally challenging structural reality in nonprofit leadership: the founder as both the organization's greatest asset and its most significant single point of failure — and the discipline required to change that dynamic.

# Chapter 13 — Founder Risk & Sustainability

## Founder Risk Is Institutional Risk

Early-stage nonprofits often revolve around a single individual.

The founder:

- Raises funds
- Designs programs
- Approves expenses
- Leads board discussions
- Communicates impact
- Carries relational capital
- Holds historical knowledge
- Absorbs emotional pressure

This feels heroic.

Structurally, it is concentration risk.

When one person becomes the system, fragility increases.

Founder dependency is not strength.
It is exposure.

Institutions that endure do not eliminate founders.
They reduce single-point-of-failure risk.

The Founder Continuity Model™ formalizes that transition.

## Visual Diagram: Founder Continuity Spectrum™

| **Stage 1** | **Stage 2** | **Stage 3** | **Stage 4** |
|---|---|---|---|
| Founder as System | Founder as Center | Founder as Architect | Founder as Steward |
| All decisions flow through founder | Most decisions require founder input | Systems run without daily founder input | Board/staff lead daily operations |
| No delegation | Some documentation | Active delegation | Full succession |

---

## The Founder Continuity Model™

Founder risk must be reduced across four dimensions:

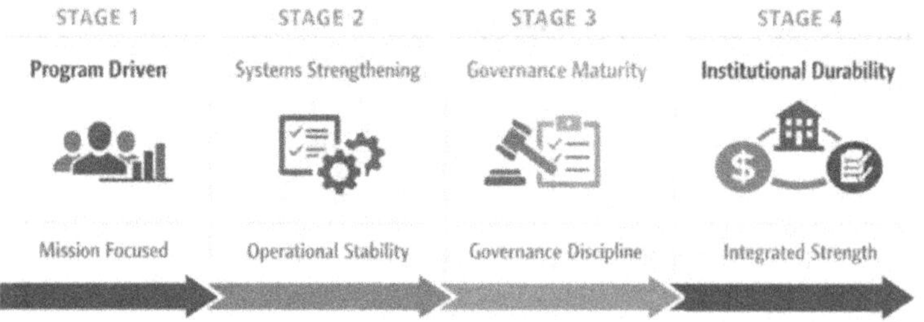


*Figure: The Four Stages of Institutional Maturity — from Founder-Centric to Institutional Governance*

1. Role Clarity
2. Authority Distribution
3. Emotional Sustainability
4. Succession Readiness

If any dimension remains underdeveloped, long-term stability is threatened.

---

# The Single-Point-of-Failure Problem™

In engineering, a single point of failure (SPOF) is a component whose failure stops the entire system.

In many nonprofits, the founder is that component.

Ask honestly:

If the founder stepped away for 90 days,
what stops?

If the answer is:
"Almost everything,"

the organization is founder-dependent.

Founder dependency is common.

## From the Field: What Vigilance Cannot Do

In December 2016, a boy named Amadou fell ill with malaria.
He was sick for several days. His mother tried a local remedy. Access to the hospital was not possible in time. He did not survive.
Word reached me by email from our colleagues in Freetown. I read it and felt the particular weight of a loss that happened inside the radius of our work, to a child we were there to help.
Develop Africa's mission at that stage was focused on education: scholarships, school supplies, computer training. We were not a health organization. We were not resourced for malaria prevention. Our mission compression, which had served us well in so many ways, had also created a shadow: we had stayed in our lane while children in the communities we served remained vulnerable to things our lane didn't cover.

After Amadou died, we expanded our scope to distribute mosquito nets to our beneficiaries. It was a direct response, narrow in its own way — not a pivot into public health, but a recognition that the children we served went home to households where preventable deaths could still happen.

This is the shadow side of mission focus that rarely appears in governance frameworks: clarity about what you will do can create a kind of institutional blindness about what happens just outside your defined boundaries. That blindness is not carelessness. It is the natural consequence of compression.

I have thought about Amadou many times since that email. Not as a failure of our organization alone, but as a reminder that our structural choices carry human consequences — even the choices that seem purely administrative. Deciding what your mission includes is also a decision about what it excludes. That deserves more than a board conversation. It deserves ongoing moral attention.

Vigilance is not a system. It's an intention. And intentions, as this book argues throughout, require structure to sustain them.

What turns vigilance into a system is simple: scope definition with embedded review. Not a mission statement that implies concern for beneficiaries — a written policy that names what the organization will monitor beyond its primary program delivery. In Develop Africa's case, after Amadou, that meant mosquito nets. A narrow addition, deliberately chosen, with a process for sourcing, distributing, and tracking them.

The lesson is not that you must expand your mission. It is that the boundaries of your mission deserve active, periodic review by your board — not just the question of what you will do, but what is happening just outside the boundary, and whether that boundary is still drawn in the right place.

Once a year, your board should ask: are the people we serve safe from the things our mission does not cover? That question will not always require a program response. But it should always require an answer.

---

# 1. Role Clarity

Founders often operate without formal job descriptions.

Responsibilities accumulate informally.

Boundaries blur.

Over time, the founder becomes:

- Executive director
- Development director
- Program manager

- HR mediator
- Financial reviewer
- Communications lead

Without clarity, overload becomes normalized.

---

## The Role Definition Rule™

Every founder should have a written role description that includes:

- Strategic responsibilities
- Operational limits
- Delegated authorities
- Reporting obligations to the board
- Decision rights boundaries

Role clarity protects:

- The founder's energy
- Staff expectations
- Board oversight
- Institutional sustainability

Without clarity, burnout accelerates silently.

---

## Mini-Example: The Invisible Role Creep

A founder begins by overseeing programs and fundraising.

Gradually, they absorb:

- Bookkeeping
- Grant reporting
- Vendor negotiation
- Staff conflict mediation
- Board coordination
- Technology troubleshooting

None of this was formally assigned.

The founder never said "no."

Over time:

- Decision fatigue increases
- Strategic thinking declines
- Delegation stalls
- Burnout intensifies

The organization did not collapse.

The founder did.

The prevention is not discipline. It is structure. Specifically: a written role description for the founder that names what is in scope and what is not — and a board that holds that boundary alongside the founder. Without a written role definition, every task that has no other owner defaults to the founder. With one, the board can ask: is this in your role? If not, who owns it? That question, asked consistently, is what transforms a founder from the organization's single point of failure into its architectural designer. Appendix E, Tool 05 — Founder Role & Boundaries — is the document that makes this concrete.

Collapse at the founder level eventually becomes institutional instability.

---

## 2. Authority Distribution

Founder-centric decision-making is efficient in early stages.

But at scale, centralization becomes a bottleneck.

Authority must gradually distribute to:

- Program leadership
- Financial oversight roles
- Board governance

- Operational managers

---

# The Authority Distribution Principle™

When authority is unclear, conflict increases.
When authority is centralized, risk increases.
When authority is distributed, stability increases.

Delegation is not loss of control.

It is structural maturity.

---

## Authority Distribution Map™

Mature institutions clearly define:

- What the board approves
- What the executive decides
- What managers control
- What requires dual authorization

Ambiguity creates dependency.

Dependency creates delay.

Delay creates frustration.

Frustration erodes culture.

---

## The Governance Reality

If the organization only works when you are present, it is not sustainable.

---

## 3. Emotional Sustainability

### The Often-Invisible Crisis

Founder sustainability is not only structural.

It is psychological.

Nonprofit leadership carries emotional load:

- Exposure to hardship
- Responsibility for beneficiaries
- Public scrutiny
- Financial uncertainty
- Crisis management
- Moral weight of decisions

Founders often internalize pressure silently.

Sacrifice culture is normalized ("If you're not exhausted, you're not committed enough").

Over time, depletion accumulates — not visibly, but consistently. The founder keeps showing up. The work continues. No one sees the internal reserve declining. Until one day, it's gone.

---

**Why This Matters for Founder Transitions**

**Most founder transitions don't happen because the founder decides to transition.**

They happen because the founder burns out.

When emotional reserves deplete:

- Decision quality declines
- Strategic patience erodes
- Founder becomes reactive instead of visionary
- Board confidence weakens
- The transition that should have been planned becomes crisis-driven

The worst founder transitions I've witnessed followed the exact same pattern:

1. Founder operates at full capacity for years

2. Multiple stressors accumulate (funding pressure, program crisis, staff conflict, personal loss)
3. Founder has no emotional reserve left to process or respond thoughtfully
4. A trigger event occurs (failed fundraising, staff departure, board criticism)
5. Founder makes a reactive decision (resignation, conflict with board, sudden pivot)
6. Organization enters crisis mode
7. Transition happens, but it's messy, damaging, and often destructive

**The transition that could have been an architecture becomes a collapse.**

---

## The Emotional Reserve Rule™

**Decision quality declines when emotional reserves are depleted.**

Exhaustion narrows perspective. Stress reduces strategic patience. Reactive decisions increase.

Defensive decisions destabilize institutions.

A founder with healthy emotional reserves:

- Can hear board feedback without defensiveness

- Can delegate without anxiety
- Can make long-term decisions despite short-term pressure
- Can support the board's independence
- Can plan their own transition calmly

A founder in emotional depletion:

- Hears board feedback as personal attack
- Cannot delegate (feels everything will collapse without them)
- Makes reactive decisions under pressure
- Perceives board oversight as threat
- Either clings to power or abandons it suddenly

**The quality of the founder transition is determined by the founder's emotional health at the time of transition.**

---

## Mini-Example: The Crisis Compounding Effect

A founder operates at full capacity for years.
Funding volatility increases stress. The founder works longer hours to compensate, personally soliciting donors.
A program setback occurs — a beneficiary is harmed, or an initiative fails. The founder internalizes responsibility.
There is no emotional reserve left. The founder cannot process the setback. Resilience is gone.

A board member raises a governance question — something that should be routine conversation.
The founder hears it as accusation. Defensiveness activates.
The response is reactive, not thoughtful.
The board member is hurt. Word spreads. Board trust declines.
The issue was not the founder's competence. It was the founder's depletion.
Within months, the founder is in conflict with the board. The board wants change; the founder digs in. The relationship breaks.

**The transition that could have been a partnership becomes a battle.**

---

**The Hidden Toll: What Burnout Costs Institutions**
Emotional depletion doesn't just harm the founder. It damages the organization:

**Burnout → Defensive Leadership**

- Founder becomes protective of authority
- Board oversight is perceived as threat
- Staff feedback is seen as disloyalty
- Risk of miscommunication increases

**Burnout → Poor Decisions**

- Strategic patience disappears
- Long-term planning stops
- Reactive firefighting increases
- Opportunities are missed

**Burnout → Isolation**

- Founder withdraws emotionally
- Peer relationships suffer
- Advisory structures atrophy
- No one sees the depletion coming

**Burnout → Sudden Departure**

- Founder resigns abruptly
- No transition plan exists
- Institutional knowledge walks out the door
- Organization enters crisis

The cost of founder burnout is not just to the founder.

It is to every person the organization serves.

---

**Emotional Sustainability Requires Deliberate Design**

Sustainability is not self-indulgence.

It is governance responsibility.

**Emotional sustainability requires:**

**1. Defined Rest Periods**

- Clear vacation policy (not just for staff — for founder too)
- Non-negotiable sabbatical every 5–7 years
- Weekly boundaries (no work on certain days/evenings)
- Actual enforcement by the board

The founder should model boundary-setting for the entire organization. If the founder works weekends and never takes vacation, the message to staff is: "Sacrifice is the price of commitment."

**2. Clear Boundaries**

- Role definition: What the founder does; what they don't
- Decision authority: Specify what decisions go to the founder; what go to staff
- Operational boundaries: Founder is not on every call, not copied on every email
- Emotional boundaries: Founder is not responsible for solving all problems

Boundaries are not selfish. They are what allow the founder to think strategically instead of react tactically.

**3. Peer Advisory Circles**

- Regular connection with other founders (or leaders in similar roles)
- Safe space to discuss challenges without judgment
- Peer perspective on founder burnout patterns
- Accountability to actually take breaks

Many founders are isolated. They carry the weight alone. A peer group is the antidote.

**4. Executive Coaching or Therapy**

- Regular reflection on emotional state
- Processing the moral weight of leadership
- Developing resilience patterns
- Identifying burnout early

This is not weakness. This is infrastructure for long-term leadership effectiveness.

**5. Structured Reflection Time**

- Regular check-ins with the board (not just about programs, but about founder wellbeing)
- Annual founder evaluation that includes emotional sustainability
- Quarterly reflection on whether the founder is hitting burnout signals
- Permission to speak up about strain

---

**The Burnout Warning Signs**

Founders should know what depletion looks like. Board members should too.

**Early warning signs of emotional depletion:**

- Increased cynicism about the work or beneficiaries
- Difficulty making decisions that would normally be routine
- Withdrawal from relationships (professional or personal)
- Increased irritability or defensiveness
- Loss of strategic thinking (everything feels urgent)
- Physical symptoms: sleep disruption, appetite changes, persistent fatigue
- Sense of futility ("Does any of this matter?")
- Inability to celebrate wins
- Constant worry about things outside your control

**These are not character flaws. They are burnout signals.**

A healthy board asks about them. A healthy founder admits them.

---

## 4. Succession Readiness

Founder sustainability extends beyond rest.

It extends into continuity.

Succession is not pessimism.

It is stewardship.

---

## The 90-Day Absence Test™

Ask:

If the founder stepped away for 90 days:

- Who communicates with donors?
- Who approves expenses?
- Who oversees program delivery?
- Who answers board inquiries?
- Who handles crisis response?

If answers are unclear, concentration risk exists.

---

## Succession Readiness Includes:

- Documented core processes
- Delegation of decision rights
- Clear second-line leadership
- Board-level contingency planning
- Knowledge transfer systems

Succession is not only about permanent departure.

It is about operational continuity under absence.

---

## The Founder Ceiling Pattern™

Many organizations plateau because:

- The founder is overloaded
- Delegation is incomplete
- Authority remains centralized
- Emotional sustainability is neglected

Growth slows not because funding is insufficient — but because leadership bandwidth is constrained.

Scaling leadership precedes scaling programs.

---

## The Transition from Founder to Architect™

In early stages, founders are operators.

At maturity, founders must become architects.

Operators execute tasks.

Architects design systems.

That transition includes:

- Designing delegation frameworks
- Accepting accountability structures
- Empowering managers
- Reducing approval centralization
- Embracing board oversight

This shift feels uncomfortable.

It is necessary.

---

# The Founder Risk Assessment™

Before declaring institutional stability, confirm:

☐ Founder role description exists
☐ Authority distribution map is documented
☐ Delegation pathways are active
☐ Financial oversight is independent

☐ Emotional recovery rhythm exists
☐ Succession contingency plan drafted
☐ Founder performance evaluation occurs annually

Unchecked items indicate concentration risk.

Concentration risk eventually surfaces.

---

## Founder Reflection

In early years, sacrifice feels necessary.

Over time, sacrifice becomes structural vulnerability.

The discipline to protect your own capacity protects the mission.

Sustainability is not selfish.

It is responsible governance.

---

Institutions outlast founders only when founders design themselves out of indispensability.

Mission begins with conviction.

Durability requires distribution.

The goal is not to be irreplaceable.

The goal is to be unnecessary to daily survival.

Founders who build systems outlast founders who carry everything alone.

## Required Outputs

By the end of this chapter, you should have — or have committed to completing within thirty days:

• A written Founder Role & Boundaries document (Tool 05, Appendix E)

• An honest answer to the 60-day test: could the organization function without you for two months?

• At least one identified successor or interim leader for your role

• A personal sustainability practice — defined rest boundaries, at least one peer relationship with another founder, and a board member you can be honest with about strain

If you have read this chapter and moved on without producing these, you have understood the doctrine and declined the work. The organization will eventually present you with the same questions under pressure. It is easier to answer them now.

*The principles are established. Chapter 14 grounds them in practice through a two-decade structural case study — tracing how one organization moved from founder-centric activity to institutional maturity across governance, finance, systems, and leadership. The patterns revealed here are not unique to one organization. They reflect the arc that durable institutions share.*

# Chapter 14 — The Develop Africa Case Study

This chapter grounds the preceding frameworks in practice — across two decades of one organization's actual financial records, governance decisions, and institutional choices. Develop Africa is not presented here as a model of perfection. It is presented as evidence: that the frameworks in this book are not theoretical. They were tested, strained, and refined across twenty years of real organizational life on two continents, beginning with the organization's current condition before tracing the choices and pressures that shaped it.

In 2025, USAID phased out significant funding streams. The funding environment became more competitive. A fundraising conference that year produced an instructive moment: an MC walked me table to table during the event, making direct asks on behalf of Develop Africa. In thirty minutes, we raised more than $600. The lesson wasn't about the technique. It was about what happens when the person asking is not the founder — when the organization's credibility can stand on its own, supported by systems and evidence, not just personality.

At this stage, Develop Africa operates with:

• Cross-border governance clarity

• Board-level dashboard reporting

• Program-level cost transparency
• Distributed leadership responsibilities
• A documented knowledge base that does not require the founder's presence to be useful

The sustainability gap remains real. Twenty years of programming data tells an honest story: organizational budgets grew from $19,639 in 2007 to a peak of $425,056 in 2022, with Form 990 figures reflecting both direct revenue and in-kind contributions in later years. The funding environment in 2025 is more competitive than it has ever been. That is not a governance failure. It is the structural reality of mission-driven work in an uncertain funding landscape.

## The Role of External Partners in Institutional Development

One of the structural decisions that shaped Develop Africa's development most significantly was the choice of external partners. This is not about donor relationships — it is about the institutional infrastructure that partners provide beyond funding.

Develop Africa joined GlobalGiving in December 2008, two years after formation. At the time, GlobalGiving was a platform for connecting donors with vetted international nonprofit projects. What it became for us was something closer to an institutional development partner.

The vetting process itself was formative. Achieving Superstar status on GlobalGiving — which requires earning top-ranked, site-visit verified, effective, and vetted badges — is not a marketing exercise. It is a governance audit. The platform's requirements for reporting cadence, outcome documentation, financial accountability, and community engagement created external accountability structures that strengthened our internal ones. The requirement to produce regular donor updates, for example, created the documentation discipline that later made our board reporting more substantive. Being donor-facing externally requires being data-ready internally.

Three members of the GlobalGiving team have visited Develop Africa's Sierra Leone operations in person — Britt Lake in May 2010, Alix Halloran in March 2017, and Dalila Sumani in May 2019. These visits were not passive. They required us to demonstrate organizational systems, partner relationships, and community accountability in real conditions. The preparation for each visit strengthened the systems we were preparing to show.

$548,659 raised through donor contributions and $309,126 driven by GlobalGiving through matching funds, grants, and prizes — a cumulative total of $857,785 through the GlobalGiving platform. The $50,000 unrestricted COVID-19 recovery grant received in 2024 — one of ten organizations selected from GlobalGiving's global cohort

— was a recognition not only of our community work but of the institutional credibility we had built over sixteen years of partnership.community work but of the institutional credibility we had built over sixteen years of partnership.

Beyond the fundraising, GlobalGiving operated as a genuine learning partner. The platform's core value — Listen, Act, Learn, Repeat — was not aspirational language. It was embedded in the Rewards system itself, which gave organizations points for stakeholder listening, program iteration, and documented learning cycles. Fundraising workshops, virtual partner visits, and a curated library of nonprofit development resources were available to every partner organization. For Develop Africa, this created a continuous improvement culture that strengthened our internal systems independently of any single campaign.

### From the Field: Responding to Ebola

*In July 2014, the World Health Organization declared the Ebola outbreak in West Africa a public health emergency of international concern. Sierra Leone was at the center of it. Schools closed. Movement was restricted. Health workers were dying.*

*Develop Africa responded on multiple fronts between July 2014 and approximately February 2015.*

*The most urgent need was personal protective equipment. Nurses and doctors at the frontline were entering wards* *without adequate protection — and contracting the virus. Without gloves, goggles, gowns, and respirators, every health worker who treated an Ebola patient was at risk of carrying the illness home. Develop Africa raised funds through a dedicated GlobalGiving Ebola project page — which received a $6,000 GlobalGiving grant in August 2014 alongside public donations and matching funds from the Paul G. Allen Foundation — and used those funds to purchase PPE in the United States, pack it into large shipment boxes, and send it to Sierra Leone. The first box was shipped by DHL on August 19, 2014. A second shipment — three large boxes of PPE and two large boxes of school supplies — departed by ocean freight on September 23, 2014.*

*In total, 27,083 units of PPE valued at $20,058.33 were delivered to Lumley Health Clinic, Blue Cross Hospital, and the Ministry of Health and Sanitation. The consignment included 909 full-body coveralls, 18,500 disposable gloves, 3,900 masks and respirators, 1,300 gowns, 1,300 aprons, 300 body bags, 400 hoods, 146 goggles, and 108 heavy-duty gloves. The delivery was received by Chief Medical Officer Dr. Brima Kargbo on August 18, 2014, and separately by Minister of Health and Sanitation Dr. Abubakar Fofanah.*

Both handovers were documented on video and are publicly accessible online. The footage shows the named government officials receiving the PPE, with GlobalGiving banners visible behind them — a level of accountability documentation that most nonprofit emergency responses do not produce.[1]

*The program was made possible through a coalition of partners: GlobalGiving Foundation and its donor community, the Paul G. Allen Foundation, the Prince of Wales Alumni Association (Georgia Chapter), the Krio Descendants Union (Georgia Chapter), and in-kind PPE contributions from Industrial Safety and Acme Prototype LLC. Develop Africa also contributed its own funds toward the response. The full funds raised through the GlobalGiving Ebola project page were pooled and disbursed based on the most urgent needs as they arose.*

*Alongside the PPE program, Develop Africa distributed soap and Dettol disinfectant in the Wellington community, provided radios and batteries to families so children could continue learning through Ministry of Education radio broadcasts, and distributed emergency food and relief supplies during the government-mandated movement restriction shutdown. Community sensitization — disseminating accurate Ebola prevention information through multiple channels — was ongoing throughout the crisis.*

---

[1] Video documentation of PPE handover to Chief Medical Officer Dr. Brima Kargbo, August 18, 2014: https://www.youtube.com/watch?v=912Ofs888R4. Video documentation of handover to Minister of Health and Sanitation Dr. Abubakar Fofanah: https://www.youtube.com/watch?v=ldYB1XE2c-c

*When the epidemic subsided, the response evolved. The twenty-two children whose parents had died became the Dream Again Home. The girls who had become pregnant during school closures and were subsequently barred from returning to mainstream education became the Educational Lifeline for Pregnant Girls. What began as an emergency response became, over three years, a series of institutional decisions about what Develop Africa was structurally equipped to carry — and what it was not.*

*Develop Africa was already a trusted GlobalGiving partner before the crisis hit — which meant donors could act immediately when the appeal went out. The lesson from the Ebola response is not only about what was accomplished. It is about the infrastructure that made it possible to act quickly. That readiness is not luck. It is the product of systems built before they were needed.*

The grants GlobalGiving provided at critical moments were equally consequential. The $30,000 emergency response grant following the 2014 Ebola outbreak made the Dream Again Home possible — twenty-two children who had lost their parents to the virus had a place to live because that grant arrived when it did. The $80,000 Ebola relief grant funded the Educational Lifeline for Pregnant Girls — a program that addressed one of the crisis's most overlooked consequences. In April 2015, Sierra Leone's Ministry of Education, Science and Technology formally banned visibly pregnant girls from attending mainstream schools and sitting national exams. The ban was actively enforced through physical searches. According to UNICEF, more than 14,000 teenage girls became pregnant during the Ebola outbreak — including 11,000 who had been in school before the crisis began. For girls already navigating trauma, loss, and stigma, the school ban compounded an already devastating situation. Develop Africa's response was direct. The Educational Lifeline for Pregnant Girls provided remedial academic instruction across core school subjects alongside psychosocial counseling — designed specifically to ensure that young women excluded from formal education did not drop out permanently. A computer lab was established to support the program. After the initial grant period, the lab was opened to the broader community, extending its reach well beyond the population it was originally designed to serve. These were not marginal contributions. They were the difference between a program existing and not existing, and between girls at risk of falling behind in their education permanently and finding a path back, and between a village having no early childhood education and having a school where thirty-six children now learn to read.

Equally important was what Superstar status unlocked beyond recognition: increased visibility on the platform, homepage and social media features, and referrals to GlobalGiving's corporate partner network. Donors who would never have encountered a Sierra Leone-focused nonprofit headquartered in Johnson City, Tennessee found us because GlobalGiving's platform put us in front of them. That kind of reach does not just change what an organization can raise. It changes what an organization is able to become.

The lesson for founders is structural: the external partners you choose impose disciplines that your internal culture may not yet generate independently. Seek partners who require you to be accountable, not just partners who provide resources. The accountability structures that feel burdensome early become competitive advantages later. Organizations that have been vetted, site-visited, and continuously evaluated by credible external partners carry a form of institutional credibility that self-reporting cannot replicate.

Develop Africa's relationship with digital giving platforms began in early 2006 — shortly after receiving our 501(c)(3) designation — when we registered on UniversalGiving.org. Founded in 2002 by Pamela Hawley and headquartered in San Francisco, UniversalGiving was at that time one of the most active international giving platforms on the web, featuring a wide range of charitable projects from organizations around the world. What distinguished it was a principle unusual for the era: the platform took no percentage of donations. One hundred percent of every gift reached the intended organization. To be listed, organizations passed a rigorous vetting process covering financial transparency, mission alignment, and leadership quality — a review that functioned as an early external credibility check for a brand-new nonprofit. UniversalGiving gave Develop Africa its first entry into peer-to-peer fundraising. Before this, our fundraising had been built on personal networks — family, friends, and immediate community. The platform opened a different door entirely: donors who had no prior relationship with us, no personal connection to Sierra Leone, and no reason to trust us except what they read on a giving page. That they gave at all was an early and important signal. Between 2006 and 2010, Develop Africa raised approximately $36,900 through the platform. Those funds supported the initial recipients of our scholarship program and contributed to the computer training programs we were delivering in Freetown. For a nonprofit in its formation years with a $23,918 first-year budget, these were not supplementary contributions. They were foundational. We owe a debt of gratitude to UniversalGiving for what they did in those early days — for giving a brand-new, diaspora-led nonprofit an opportunity to be seen, to be trusted, and to grow. The lesson it taught us was structural: the moment you move from fundraising within your personal network to fundraising on a platform, you have crossed a threshold. Strangers are now deciding whether your organization deserves their trust. That requires a different kind of accountability — one that is documented, transparent, and legible to people who have never met you.

In December 2013, Develop Africa joined Google One Today — a mobile application launched by Google that year to connect donors with vetted nonprofits through daily micro-giving. The model was elegantly simple: users could donate as little as one dollar per day to a featured project. Google covered all processing fees, meaning one hundred percent of every donation reached the nonprofit. Funds were distributed through Network for Good, which provided both the payment infrastructure and annual tax receipts to donors. Organizations were required to be validated through Google for Nonprofits before joining, adding an additional layer of external credibility verification.

I came across the app because of my technology background — a willingness to engage with new platforms early. I created multiple projects on the app, having learned that different appeals speak to different donors. An appeal for school supplies resonates differently than an appeal for mosquito nets. Someone who has never needed to sleep under a net understands school supplies immediately. Listing projects across a range of needs meant reaching a wider range of people. We began receiving donations from strangers who had found our projects through the app — people who had never heard of Develop Africa, discovered us through a mobile platform, and gave.

Between 2013 and 2020, Develop Africa raised approximately $60,700 through Google One Today. These funds went to the specific projects donors selected — school supplies, scholarships, computer training — and helped sustain programming during years when other funding was inconsistent. In January 2020, Google announced that the app would shut down on February 6, giving nonprofits less than two weeks' notice. It was a genuine loss. The platform had given Develop Africa access to donors who would never otherwise have found us.

The lesson is structural: technology platforms are seasonal. They open, they grow, they close. The organizations that benefit most are those that adopt early, before the crowd arrives, and extract maximum value before the season ends. That is not a technology lesson. It is a governance lesson about organizational responsiveness to opportunity.

A personal word is warranted here. Develop Africa would not be where it is today without GlobalGiving. That is not a polite acknowledgment. It is an institutional fact.

The platform gave us visibility we could not have generated on our own, access to donors who would never otherwise have heard of a Sierra Leone-focused nonprofit in Johnson City, Tennessee, and a giving infrastructure that a small diaspora-led organization could not have built independently. The training sessions, the webinars, the learning resources, the vetting process — all of it made us better. The site visits from GlobalGiving staff — three of them, across very different seasons of our organizational life — validated our work in ways that donor reports alone cannot. And the grants they provided at moments of genuine crisis — for PPE during Ebola, for the Educational Lifeline for Pregnant Girls, for the Dream Again Home — made programs possible that would not otherwise have existed.

We owe GlobalGiving a debt of gratitude that this book can only partially repay by documenting what the partnership made possible. They nurtured us when we were new, encouraged us when the work was hard, and gave others a reason to trust us before we had fully earned that trust on our own. For that, we are forever grateful.

*The institutional credibility you earn through external vetting is not merely a fundraising asset. It is structural proof that your organization functions as represented — that your governance is real, your programs are accountable, and your reporting is honest. In a sector where self-certification is the norm, third-party validation is the exception. Pursue it deliberately.*

What has changed is this: the organization can navigate that uncertainty with systems that do not depend on any single person's stamina or presence.

## The Structural Condition at Stage Four

Role Clarity: Founder role defined strategically, not operationally.
Authority Distribution: Managers and board leaders operate with delegated clarity.
Emotional Sustainability: Pressure is shared rather than absorbed.
Succession Readiness: Processes are documented. Leadership depth exists beyond one individual.

## Eight Lessons Across Twenty Years

These are not principles developed in retrospect to seem wise. They are observations from the actual experience of building Develop Africa — lessons that emerged from specific moments, specific failures, and specific choices.

1. The founder's credibility is the organization's first infrastructure. Before there are systems, there is trust. Donors give because they trust the person asking. Partners engage because they believe in the person leading. That credibility is not a liability to be designed away — it is the foundation on which systems are eventually built. Protect it with integrity.

2. Single points of failure will reveal themselves. The question is whether you discover them through deliberate

audit or through disruption. A staircase in Freetown taught me this more clearly than any management book.

3. The first SOP is usually written because of a departure. The departure of Grace forced the first documented financial procedure in our history. Don't wait for the departure. Write the process now, while the person who knows it is still present.

4. Narrow mission focus has a shadow side. Compression is essential for governance. But the decision about what your mission includes is also a decision about what it excludes. That boundary carries human consequences. It deserves more than a strategy conversation.

5. Systems are institutional memory. The knowledge base I built did not replace relationships or judgment. It preserved context that would otherwise have lived only in my head. Memory stored in structure does not retire or burn out.

6. Governance legitimizes authority; it does not diminish it. The executive session felt like a threat to my role until I understood it as evidence that my role was real enough to require independent oversight. Governance is not surveillance. It is the architecture that makes authority credible.

7. The founder's personal growth is organizational

infrastructure. The board that introduces executive session, the founder who accepts it, the leader who builds a knowledge base not because they were asked to but because they understand why — that kind of growth is not personal development. It is structural investment.

8. The transition from founder to steward is the hardest and most important work. Not because it requires giving anything up, but because it requires building something durable enough that giving it up would actually be possible. That is the work this book has been pointing toward from the first chapter.

In the early years, I believed that the depth of my commitment to this work was a sufficient structural foundation. It was not. Commitment initiates. Structure sustains.

The girl on Howe Street is a grown woman now, wherever she is. I don't know what became of her specifically. What I know is that the work started because of her — and that it has endured not because of the intensity of that original moment, but because of the machinery built around it in the years since.

Build machinery worthy of the heart that moved you to start.

That is what institutions are for.

## From the Field: What We Assumed They Understood

Over the years, Develop Africa has worked with several implementing partner organizations. In one specific case, I made an assumption I didn't know I was making. I assumed that because we had articulated our procedures and preferences clearly, our partners understood it the same way we did.

I assumed that because we had articulated our model clearly to ourselves, our partners understood it the same way we did.

They didn't. Not entirely. There was a situation where the leadership of a partner organization decided to go in a different direction than we had agreed on with respect to engagement with a government unit. We agreed on one direction. When the meeting between the organization and the unit took place, the partner went a different direction without informing us. Perhaps there was a very good reason for their decision to do so. However, this was not communicated to us. This raised a red flag. The relationship eventually ended for other reasons.

That breakdown wasn't about bad intentions on anyone's part. It was partly about the absence of written agreements that specified who communicated what, to whom, and under what authority. Meetings and discussions were not adequately documented. A shared verbal understanding is not a governance structure. It is an assumption waiting to be tested. Many good intentions have failed because of the lack of documentation. Not having documentation can also result in misinterpretation.

The lesson from that partnership is not that external partners cannot be trusted. It is that trust requires structure to sustain it across distance, across cultures, and across different institutional priorities. The partner organization was possibly not wrong to go in a different direction. But we had not built a written framework that clarified whose decision it was to make.

Before entering any significant partnership — especially one that crosses organizational, cultural, or geographic lines — three things must be written down: who has authority to make which decisions, how disagreements will be resolved, and what the exit looks like if the partnership ends. Not because you expect any of those situations. Because the absence of answers, when they are needed, is exactly what creates the breakdown.

Currency and Cash Flow: USD held in Tennessee moves differently than local currency in Freetown. Exchange rates shift. Wire transfer timing introduces delay. Your financial oversight must account for this operational reality.

Cultural Communication Norms: Directness valued in one culture reads as harsh in another. Decision-making interpreted as consensus in one context becomes stalling in another. Written agreements replace assumption.

Regulatory Differences: A U.S. 501(c)(3) does not exist in Sierra Leone. Local NGO registration, tax obligations, and reporting timelines differ. Your governance must accommodate both simultaneously.

When your organization operates across borders, governance complexity multiplies. Three dimensions require explicit attention:

**SIDEBAR: Cross-Border Governance Considerations**

Cross-border and cross-organization work multiplies this problem. Different cultural contexts carry different norms around authority, communication, and decision-making. What one party experiences as a natural next step, another may experience as overreach. Written agreements don't eliminate those differences. But they create a shared reference point that verbal alignment cannot.

We learned to require written memoranda of understanding for every partnership — specifying roles, communication authority, reporting obligations, and decision boundaries. Not because we distrusted our partners, but because **trust without documentation is fragile under pressure.**

This principle applies to all partnerships, not just international ones. When pressure arrives — when timelines tighten, when misunderstandings surface, when stakes rise — documented agreements become the architecture under pressure.

Scaling into new geographies or new partnerships requires more documentation, not less. The temptation is to move fast and formalize later. That instinct has a cost.

---

## November 2025

In November 2025, I visited Kamawornie for the first time.

I had known Kamawornie for years through photographs, donor reports, and staff updates. A fellow US board member had visited the village before the COVID-19 pandemic. I had not. So when I finally walked into the community — past the elders gathered under large trees, past the mothers and youth who had assembled to receive us — I was seeing faces I already recognized. I had just never stood in front of them before.

The nursery school was there. A building. Classrooms with children at small desks, a teacher at the front of each room, painted walls, windows letting in light. The children sang welcome songs. They were curious and unself-conscious. The teachers spoke openly about their work — the training they had received, the materials they had been given, the difference it had made in what they could offer to the children in front of them.

Before Develop Africa's involvement, Kamawornie had no early childhood education. Children entered Class One without foundational skills. There was no structured pathway. There was nothing to build on.

The construction was made possible in part through a dedicated GlobalGiving fundraising campaign. The initial funds that broke ground came from donors who found the project through the platform. Construction began in February 2022, reached roof height by end of year, and was completed in late 2023. The official opening ceremony took place on February 9, 2024, attended by local dignitaries including the Member of Parliament Honorable Amend Kargbo, Deputy Director of Education Ibrahim S. Tawarallie, and a representative from the Ministry of Gender and Children Affairs. Thirty-six students enrolled in the first cohort. The school serves a community where, before its construction, children entered Class One with no early childhood foundation — and where mothers had previously had no option but to carry young children to their farms because there was nowhere else for them to go. That problem has been solved. A building, three classrooms, desks, chairs, blackboards, a bathroom, a fence, and a playground now stand in Kamawornie village. They stand in part because GlobalGiving donors believed in a project they found on a platform — and gave.

The elders asked that a message be carried back to our donors: a sincere thank-you for believing in this village and investing consistently in its children's future. I told them I would carry it. I am carrying it now.

### From the Field: The Year of the Pencil

*On November 20, 2025 — World Children's Day — Develop Africa, in partnership with the Freetown City Council and the GEED Foundation, distributed 100,000 pencils, 10,000 learning pouches, and 10,000 sharpeners to 10,000 pupils across twenty primary schools in Freetown, Sierra Leone. The slogan was simple: A Pencil Today, A Brighter Tomorrow.*

*The official launch was held at Regent Square Municipal Infant Primary School, where Freetown Mayor Yvonne Aki-Sawyerr personally handed out the first set of pouches to pupils. The school alone received supplies for 626 pupils —*

*10 pencils and one sharpener each. The Mayor applauded the initiative and emphasized how timely and impactful the distribution was in supporting the educational growth of the city's children. Her words put into plain terms what the data confirmed:*

> *"From Nursery 2 to Class 3, many children come to school without a pencil. Their parents cannot always afford basic supplies. This campaign gives them a fair chance to learn, write, and participate."*

*— Mayor Yvonne Aki-Sawyerr, Freetown City Council*

*Each of the 10,000 pouches had been packed by hand by the Develop Africa Sierra Leone team in the days before the distribution. Deliveries were made simultaneously across all twenty schools on the same day. The Sierra Leone Broadcasting Corporation covered the event, amplifying the campaign's reach beyond the school gates.*

*Teachers at schools across Freetown described what the supplies meant in practical terms. At one school, a head teacher explained that students frequently arrive without anything to write with and must request pencils from the teacher — disrupting lessons and undermining the child's sense of readiness. One pupil, receiving her pouch, said: "I feel ready for school now. I don't have to borrow anymore."*

*The governance lesson from the Year of the Pencil is not about scale. It is about partnership architecture. A program of this size — twenty schools, one day, 100,000 units — required institutional coordination that Develop Africa could not have executed alone. The Freetown City Council provided distribution infrastructure and official presence. The GEED Foundation contributed resources and coordination. Develop Africa provided program design, supply logistics, and accountability documentation. Each partner brought what the others lacked. That is what mature institutional partnerships look like. Not one organization doing everything. Three organizations doing what each does best.*

*A pencil is small. The opportunity it represents is not. Develop Africa began in 2006 with a computer training program projected onto a bedsheet in Freetown. Nearly two decades later, the organization delivered 100,000 pencils to 10,000 children in a single day — with the Mayor of Freetown standing in the schoolyard, handing them out by hand. That arc is not an accident. It is the result of systems built to carry weight that passion alone cannot.*

What I saw in Kamawornie was not a project. It was an institution — small by any external measure, but real. It had structure, continuity, and community ownership. It did not require my presence to function. It required the twenty years of organizational infrastructure that made it possible for someone to build it, and for someone else to sustain it, long before I arrived.

That is what this case study is ultimately about. Not the founding moment, not the founder's commitment, not the depth of the original vision — but the machinery built over decades that allowed a classroom to open in a remote village in Sierra Leone and still be standing, and still be full of children, when the founder finally came to see it.

## Founder Toolkit — Apply the Case Study to Your Organization

The Develop Africa case study is most useful when it becomes a mirror. After reading this chapter, ask five questions about your own organization:

1. At what governance stage are we currently operating — honestly?

2. What is the gap between our financial reporting and what our board actually needs to govern well?

3. Where have we expanded beyond our capacity in the past two years?

4. What institutional knowledge lives only in the founder's head?

5. If the founder left tomorrow, what would stop?

Tool 10 — Governance Maturity Scoring Worksheet provides the structured instrument for answering question one with your board. Tool 11 — Governance Maturity 12-Month Roadmap translates that answer into a concrete next-steps plan.

→ Appendix E, Tool 10 | Tool 11 — www.missiontosystems.com/tools

What the case study confirms is what the preceding chapters have argued: durability follows a pattern. Chapter 15 codifies that pattern into five structural laws.

# Chapter 15 — The Doctrine of Institutional Durability

## From the Field: Still Standing

After the governance gaps of the early years. After the Dream Again Home. After the microfinance program. After Amadou. After the USAID phase-outs of 2025. Nov 2025: Year of the Pencil campaign. 100,000 pencils, 10,000 pouches, and 10,000 sharpeners distributed to 10,000 pupils across 20 schools in Freetown, in partnership with Freetown City Council and GEED Foundation. Mayor Yvonne Aki-Sawyerr attends launch.

Institutional durability is not a concept I learned from a book. It is something Develop Africa has had to demonstrate — repeatedly, across different kinds of seasons, against different kinds of pressure.

What does it mean? Not the definition. The feeling.

It means being able to take a licking and keep ticking. It means weathering the storm without knowing when the storm ends. It means pivoting when the path closes, contracting when the season demands it, finding efficiency you didn't know you had because you had no other choice.

When USAID phased out significant funding streams in 2025, we had to contract. We did. We are still here. In this season we are more disciplined, more efficient, and more creative than we have ever been. We are seeking additional sources of income and leveraging the relationships and experience built over two decades. We are not waiting for conditions to improve. We are building the conditions ourselves.

Durability also means knowing the difference between a difficult season and a finished one. Not every organization that struggles is dying. Some are simply being tested — and the test is whether the structure you built is strong enough to hold through pressure that the mission alone cannot absorb.

That is what this chapter is about. Not inspiration. Architecture.

## The Structural Plateau

Between initiative and institution lies a plateau.

Organizations that cross the plateau become structure-driven.

Those that do not remain personality-driven.

---

**Structural Laws That Outlast Founders**

Institutions do not endure by intention.
They endure by design.

Across organizations that survive leadership transitions, funding volatility, and public scrutiny, recurring structural patterns emerge.

These are not motivational principles.
They are observable realities.

Organizations delay them.
They do not escape them.

What follows are five structural laws of durability.

# Law I

# Clarity Precedes Capacity

Capacity does not create clarity.

Clarity creates capacity.

Before an organization can scale, fundraise effectively, document systems, or govern responsibly, it must define:

- The problem it solves
- The population it serves

- The change it produces
- The cost of producing that change

Unclear problems produce unclear programs.
Unclear programs produce unstable funding.
Unstable funding produces reactive leadership.

Clarity is not branding language.

It is operational precision.

Organizations that expand without clarity introduce complexity faster than discipline can absorb it.

Durable institutions define first.
Then they build.

---

## Law II

## Governance Protects the Mission

Governance is not ceremonial.

It is structural risk management.

When governance is passive:

- Authority becomes ambiguous

- Accountability becomes personal
- Oversight weakens
- Risk concentrates
- Founder dependency increases

Strong governance does not eliminate risk.

It distributes it responsibly.

Durable institutions maintain:

- Defined board authority
- Financial oversight independent of execution
- Executive evaluation discipline
- Documented approval flows
- Predictable reporting cadence

You can survive without governance for a season.

It will not mature without it.

---

# Law III

# Systems Outlive Energy

Founder intensity can initiate momentum.

It cannot preserve it.

Systems convert effort into repeatable structure.

A system is not a document.
It is a repeatable sequence that survives personnel change.

When approvals, program delivery, reporting, and communication depend on memory or stamina, fragility increases.

Durable institutions:

- Write processes down
- Clarify authority boundaries
- Document handoffs
- Standardize financial workflows
- Define communication rhythm

Systems reduce personality dependency.

If your organization cannot function without you, it is not yet durable.

It is exposed.

---

# Law IV

# Transparency Compounds Trust

Trust is not earned through perfection.

It is earned through consistency.

Organizations that report only success create credibility risk.

Organizations that communicate irregularly erode confidence silently.

Durable institutions practice:

- Predictable communication cadence
- Honest reporting of challenges
- Financial explainability
- Outcome measurement discipline
- Governance visibility

Trust compounds slowly.

It erodes quickly.

Funding follows trust more reliably than persuasion.

Transparency is not vulnerability.

It is structural strength.

---

# Law V

# Scaling Magnifies Structure

Growth does not correct weakness.

It exposes it.

An unclear approval process becomes chaotic under expansion.
A passive board becomes dangerous at scale.
A founder-dependent model becomes unstable under funding growth.

Scaling multiplies what already exists.

If structure is strong, growth increases impact.
If structure is weak, growth increases strain.

Before expansion, durable institutions ask:

- Are systems documented?
- Is governance active?
- Is financial oversight explainable?
- Is authority distributed?
- Can leadership operate without founder centrality?

When growth is intentional, institutions strengthen.
When growth is impulsive, institutions fracture.

# The Founder Continuity Imperative

Every durable institution eventually reduces concentration risk.

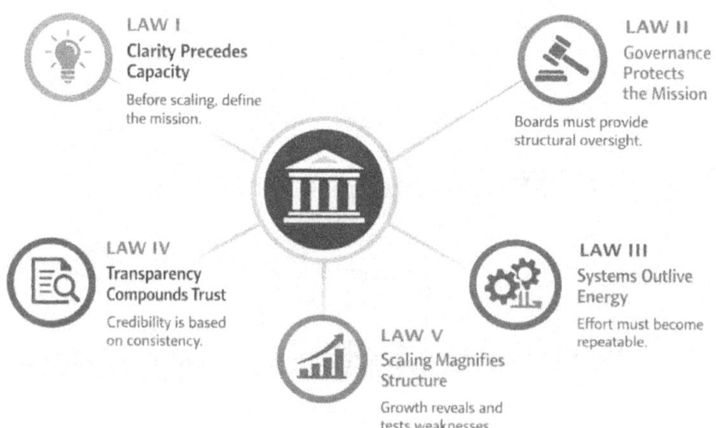


\Founder dependence is natural early.

It is dangerous long-term.

Durability requires:

- Role clarity

- Authority distribution
- Emotional sustainability
- Succession readiness

An institution that depends on one individual's stamina is not resilient.

It is temporary.

Designing oneself out of indispensability is not abandonment.

It is stewardship.

---

# Institutional Readiness Defined

An institution is durable when:

- Its mission is clear without explanation from the founder
- Its board governs with defined authority
- Its finances are explainable without hesitation
- Its programs operate through documented systems
- Its communication withstands scrutiny
- Its leadership is transferable

Durability is not size.

It is proportional discipline.

---

Good intentions do not preserve institutions.

Structure does.

Activity does not equal maturity.

Growth does not equal durability.

Passion does not replace governance.

Energy does not replace systems.

---

Mission inspires.

Structure sustains.

Governance protects.

Systems preserve.

Transparency legitimizes.

Distributed leadership stabilizes.

Durability is the cumulative result of disciplined design.

Institutions outlast founders only when leadership chooses structure over improvisation, clarity over ego, and stewardship over control.

This is not theory.

It is structural law.

## Required Outputs

By the end of this chapter — and this book — you should be able to answer five questions honestly:

1. Can your organization operate for 60 days without you?

2. Are your five core systems documented and owned by someone other than the founder?

3. Does your board govern independently — or does it govern through you?

4. Does your financial reporting give your board actual oversight — or the appearance of it?

5. Have you designed a succession path, however preliminary?

These are not aspirations. They are the structural tests that determine whether this book changed anything for your organization. If you can answer yes to all five, the doctrine has been implemented. If you cannot, you have identified your next priorities. Either answer is useful. Avoidance is the only response that costs you.

> ## Founder Toolkit — Document Your Role Before It Becomes a Crisis
>
> Most founders do not address role boundaries until a board conflict, a health crisis, or a key staff departure forces the question. By then, the cost is higher than it needed to be.
>
> The Founder Role & Boundaries document exists to make the implicit explicit — while you still have the clarity and the margin to be honest.
>
> → **Appendix E, Tool 05 — Founder Role & Boundaries**

*The doctrine is established. What remains is the decision to build accordingly.*

# Epilogue

# From Founder to Architect

In the beginning, most institutions are carried by intensity.

The founder moves quickly.
Decisions are immediate.
Energy compensates for structure.
Commitment substitutes for documentation.

This phase is necessary.

But it is not durable.

Over time, the question changes.

It is no longer:

"How do we grow?"

It becomes:

"How do we endure?"

That shift marks the transition from founder to architect.

---

## The Operator Phase

Operators execute.

They respond to need without pause.

They solve problems as they appear.

They fill gaps.

They carry the organization forward through will.

Operators are essential.

But they are not architects.

## The Architect Phase

Architects design systems that outlast their own involvement.

They do not solve every problem personally.

They build structures so that others can solve problems consistently.

They do not hold institutional knowledge privately.

They distribute it intentionally.

They do not depend on being indispensable.

They design themselves out of necessity.

This transition is rarely comfortable.

It requires relinquishing control that once felt protective.

It requires accepting accountability structures that once felt unnecessary.

It requires trusting others with work that once felt personal.

But it is the most important structural decision a founder makes.

The chapters behind you trace what that decision looks like in practice — and what it produces.

*The Institutional Maturity Imperative*

## Most Missions Never Become Institutions

They begin with clarity. They grow through passion. They stall through fragility. The nonprofit landscape is filled with good intentions that never matured into durable institutions — not because the mission lacked value, but because structure never caught up to aspiration.

*Mission is inspiration. Institution is endurance. Mission starts movements. Institutions outlast founders.*

## The Maturity Arc

Throughout this book, we have walked the arc: Problem Clarity → Mission Definition → Structural Choice → Legal Foundation → Governance Formation → Program Architecture → Financial Discipline → Fundraising Readiness → Operational Systems → Evaluation

Consistency → Trust Architecture → Scaling Discipline → Founder Sustainability. Each layer protects the next. Skip layers — instability grows. Honor layers — resilience builds.

## The Institutional Maturity Imperative

The question is no longer: "Can we start?" It becomes: "Can we endure?" Endurance requires: clarity over charisma, systems over improvisation, governance over personality, transparency over perception, and discipline over momentum. Endurance is engineered. It is not accidental.

## The Structural Plateau

Between initiative and institution lies a plateau where governance lags growth. Organizations that push through it deliberately become structure-driven. Those that do not remain fragile.

## The Compounding Effect

When structure strengthens: trust compounds, partnerships deepen, board confidence stabilizes, donor renewal increases, and staff retention improves. Institutional maturity reduces volatility. Volatility reduction increases confidence. Confidence attracts stability. Stability sustains mission.

## Institutional Resilience Defined

An institution is resilient when leadership transitions do not destabilize operations, funding fluctuations do not threaten payroll, program setbacks trigger learning rather than crisis, and governance challenges resolve through process rather than personality. Resilience is visible during pressure. Pressure reveals maturity.

## Founder Reflection

At some point, every founder must confront a quiet question: Is this organization dependent on me — or disciplined beyond me? The transition from founder-centric to system-centric is the moment a nonprofit becomes an institution. That shift is not emotional. It is structural. It requires humility. It requires discipline. It requires trust in governance. But once achieved, the mission becomes durable.

## The Institutional Readiness Test

Before claiming maturity, confirm:

- ☐ Governance functions independently.
- ☐ Financial reporting is explainable.
- ☐ Systems operate without founder intervention.
- ☐ Communication cadence is predictable.
- ☐ Program outcomes are measured consistently.
- ☐ Scaling decisions are disciplined.
- ☐ Succession pathways exist.

*If these conditions are present, you are no longer building a nonprofit. You are stewarding an institution.*

## Value-Aligned Institutional Rules

If you value stewardship → Build beyond yourself.

If you value integrity → Make systems visible.

If you value accountability → Welcome governance oversight.

If you value sustainability → Strengthen structure before scale.

If you value trust → Practice transparency consistently.

If you value impact → Protect the architecture that delivers it.

## The Core Principle

## Things fall apart when systems are absent. When systems are present, things endure. This is not pessimism. It is structural realism.

## A Closing Thought

Mission without systems inspires briefly. Mission with systems transforms persistently. You do not honor your cause by moving fast. You honor it by building well.

Because good intentions begin missions. But systems create institutions. And institutions outlive exhaustion.

# The Institutional Readiness Oath

*A Commitment to Structural Stewardship*

*Before growth. Before scale. Before recognition.*

**We commit to structure.**

We affirm that mission alone is not enough. We understand that intention without systems creates fragility. We recognize that trust must be engineered — not assumed. We accept that governance protects the mission.

We commit to financial discipline — even when no one is watching. We will document processes so knowledge does not live in one person. We will measure outcomes so impact can be explained. We will scale only when structure supports it. We will choose durability over speed. We will choose clarity over charisma. We will choose accountability over convenience. We will build institutions — not personalities.

We understand that structure is not bureaucracy. It is the architecture of mission survival.

We commit to building systems. We commit to strengthening governance. We commit to institutional maturity — not for recognition, not for optics, but for endurance.

*Because the mission deserves more than momentum.*

**It deserves resilience.**

# A Final Word

*And Your Next Step*

I did not write this book from theory.

I wrote it from experience.

From systems that failed because they were never documented. From board structures that were unclear. From funding cycles that exposed structural weakness. From growth that stretched leadership faster than governance could support. From seasons that demanded more discipline than passion could provide.

Over time, one principle became undeniable:

> **Things fall apart when systems are absent.**

Not loudly. Not instantly. But predictably.

Organizations that neglect these structural laws do not fail dramatically. They fail quietly. They stall. They plateau. They become permanent startups staffed by people who are exhausted from carrying systems in their heads.

**Mission to Systems™ is not a slogan.** It is a standard.

A standard for how institutions mature. A standard for how governance protects mission. A standard for how trust compounds.

If you have read this far, you are not looking for inspiration.

You are looking for durability.

And durability requires structure.

## If You Are Ready to Go Further

This book is the doctrine. But doctrine must be implemented.

If you are ready to go further, here is what that looks like:

- The Mission to Systems™ Core Video Course
- Governance Maturity Scoring
- Strategic Advisory for Boards and Founders

Each offering is designed to move from knowledge to execution — from understanding to measurable structural maturity.

Because reading about systems is not the same as building them.

The question is no longer:

*Can you start?*

The question is:

***Will your mission endure?***

Build slow. Build disciplined. Build governable. Build transferable. Build resilient.

The mission deserves more than momentum.

**It deserves structure.**

— *Sylvester Renner*

Founder, Develop Africa | Creator, Mission to Systems™

sylrenner.com | www.missiontosystems.com

MISSION TO SYSTEMS™

# Mission inspires. Structure endures. Institutions outlast intention.

— *Sylvester Renner*

**MISSION TO SYSTEMS™ | Governance. Structure. Endurance.**

# Appendix A — Twenty Years of Institutional Development: What It Looks Like in the Numbers

Governance frameworks describe how institutions should be built. Financial records show whether they were. The table below reflects Develop Africa's annual budget as reported on IRS Form 990/990-EZ from 2006 through 2024 — twenty years of real institutional development, in real dollars, through real conditions.

These are not projections or estimates. They are the audited financial record of one organization's journey from formation to institutional maturity. The numbers reflect scholarship distributions, computer training programs, school supplies, solar lights, Ebola response, the Dream Again Home orphanage, nursery school construction, and all the administrative and governance infrastructure required to sustain those programs with accountability.

Read this table not as a success narrative but as a structural document. Notice where growth stalled (2011 to 2013), where it accelerated (2014 to 2016, driven by the two GlobalGiving Ebola relief grants totaling $110,000), where it plateaued (2018 to 2020), and where it reached its current scale. Notice that the 2025 funding environment — shaped by USAID phase-outs and increased competition — is not visible in this table but is real. Growth lines on financial records do not capture the institutional discipline required to survive the seasons between the high points.

The governance principles in this book were not written about this data. They were written from it.

DEVELOP AFRICA — ANNUAL BUDGET (IRS FORM 990/990-EZ)

| Year | Budget | Notes |
|---|---|---|
| 2005 | — | EIN obtained from IRS |
| 2006 | $23,918 | Formation year. IRS registration April 2006. First programs delivered. |
| 2007 | $19,639 | Program growth |
| 2008 | $19,068 | First office lease (September 2008). |
| 2009 | $27,049 | Early growth. UniversalGiving active. |
| 2010 | $91,952 | Platform expansion. First site visit. |
| 2011 | $60,520 | Plateau. Systems under strain. |
| 2012 | $110,310 | Grace departure. First SOP written. |
| 2013 | $75,867 | Mid-plateau. Governance gaps visible. |
| 2014 | $181,172 | First real board minutes. DASL launch. |
| 2015 | $256,182 | Ebola response scaling. |
| 2016 | $185,531 | Post-Ebola contraction. |
| 2017 | $198,395 | Dream Again Home phase-out begins. |
| 2018 | $230,657 | Dream Again Home phase-out complete. 18/21 placed. |
| 2019 | $195,740 | Stable operations. Second site visit. |
| 2020 | $223,462 | COVID. Fundraising contraction. |
| 2021 | $354,162 | Recovery. Google One Today active. |
| 2022 | $425,056 | Peak budget to date. |
| 2023 | $316,100 | Funding environment shifts. |
| 2024 | $404,644 | Kamawornie nursery school opens. |

Total (2006-2024): approximately $3.4 million

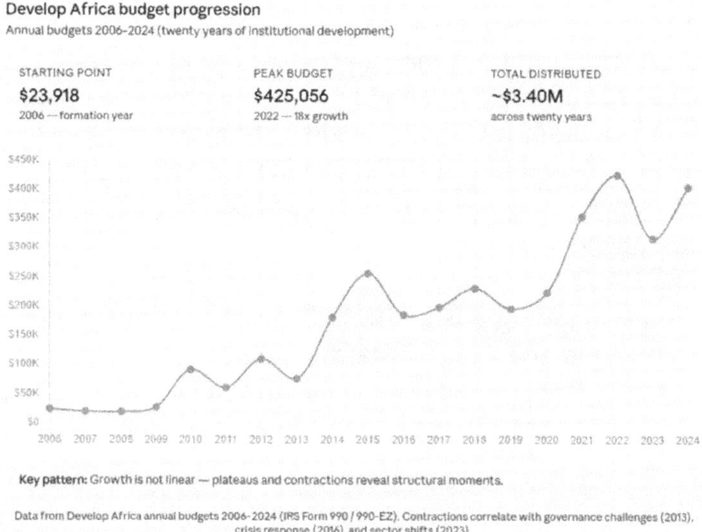


Three observations are worth drawing from this record.

First, growth is not linear. The budget dropped from $91,952 in 2010 to $60,520 in 2011 — a 34% contraction — before more than doubling by 2012. It dropped again in 2013, then nearly tripled by 2015. Organizations that present only peak-year numbers misrepresent the experience of institutional development. The plateaus and contractions are where governance is tested. They are where systems either hold or collapse.

Second, the inflection points correlate with structural decisions, not just fundraising success. The 2014 jump corresponded to the first real board meeting with minutes and the launch of Develop Africa Sierra Leone — structural investments, not campaign wins. The 2021 recovery followed years of internal systems work during COVID, not simply an improved fundraising environment.

Third, scale does not resolve governance. The same governance questions that confronted Develop Africa at $19,000 confronted us at $425,056 — with higher stakes and less margin for error. The discipline required to be accountable at small scale is identical to the discipline required to be accountable at large scale. The difference is consequence.

If you are reading this in the early years of your organization, the $23,918 starting point is not the point of this table. The point is what came after it — and what had to be built, corrected, and rebuilt to get from there to here.

# Appendix B — Develop Africa: Institutional Milestone Timeline

The chapters of this book move through governance principles sequentially. This timeline moves through the same territory chronologically — the actual sequence of events, decisions, and structural moments that produced the organization described in this book. Read alongside the 990 budget table in Appendix A, it gives the fullest picture of what twenty years of institutional development actually looked like as it was happening.

PHASE I: CATALYST & FORMATION (2003–2006)

2003 Catalyst moment. Howe Street, Freetown, Sierra Leone.
A young girl crouching on the pavement asking for food.
The mission begins as a problem Sylvester Renner cannot ignore.

Oct 2005 Decision made to launch Develop Africa. Co-founded with a fellow Sierra Leonean.
Application submitted for Employer Identification Number (EIN).

Dec 7, 2005 EIN registered and obtained from IRS.
First bank account opened. Registered on UniversalGiving.org.

Jan 30, 2006 Develop Africa incorporated with the State of Tennessee as a nonprofit. Foundation Group facilitates filing. Cost: ~$1,600.

Apr 13, 2006 Registration approved by the Division of Charitable Solicitation and Gaming, State of Tennessee.

Apr 26, 2006 Letter of Determination received from IRS. Develop Africa formally recognized as tax-exempt 501(c)(3) by the IRS.

Cost: approximately $1,600. Five-member founding board seated: Sylvester Renner, Co-founder, George (Kenya), Henry (education), Janet (Sierra Leone / Fourah Bay College classmate).

2006 First funds raised. Books and school supplies collected in founder's basement. First scholarships distributed in Sierra Leone.

Dec 2006 First program delivered: computer training at iEARN Sierra Leone,

Stadium Hostel, Freetown. Bedsheet as screen. Projector on books. Candlelight when power cut. 12 participants. Programs before funding.

## PHASE II: EARLY GROWTH & PARTNER BUILDING (2007–2013)

Sep 2008 First office space leased in Tennessee. Organization moves out of the founder's basement into institutional infrastructure.

Dec 2008 Develop Africa joins GlobalGiving. Partnership begins that will generate over $1.1M in funding over 18 years.

2009 Founder falls on stairs in Sierra Leone. Pulled back muscle. 2-3 months of impaired capacity. Programs stall. First encounter with the cost of founder-centric operations. Budget: $27,049.

2009-2013 Expansion to partners in Cameroon, Ivory Coast, Ethiopia, Gambia, and Kenya. Country diversification phase.

Door of Hope, founded by Joshua Sandy (Wellington, Freetown), becomes primary ground partner,

introduced by Janet. Mosquito nets, scholarships, solar lights, tailoring school, Ebola sensitization, FAWE Computer Lab.

May 2010 First GlobalGiving site visit. Britt Lake visits Sierra Leone. Budget reaches $91,952 — largest to date.

2011 Budget drops to $60,520. Systems under strain. Structural plateau becomes visible. Board governance informal. No minutes discipline.

~2012 Grace (admin assistant, Tri-Cities) departs. Organization forced to write its first real SOP — Network for Good donor acknowledgment.

### From the Field: Choosing and Keeping a Donation Platform

*Over the years, Develop Africa has used several different donation platforms as its primary fundraising channel. Each transition taught us something. Taken together, they produced two governance principles that any nonprofit selecting a platform should apply before signing up.*

*The first principle is the must-have test. Before evaluating any platform, identify the features your organization absolutely cannot operate without. For Develop Africa, child sponsorship functionality was a must-have. Donors who sponsor a specific child expect to be connected to that child's progress over time — they want updates, photos, and a relationship, not just a receipt. Not every platform supports that model. Any platform that does not have your must-haves is eliminated from consideration regardless of its other features, its pricing, or the quality of its sales pitch. This sounds obvious. It is not consistently practiced.*

*The second principle is the switching cost. Every time you move donors from one platform to another, you ask them to re-register, update their payment information, and re-establish their giving habit. Some do. Some do not. Develop Africa has lost donors at every platform transition — donors who were considering canceling anyway and used the friction of the switch as the moment to stop. Platform stability is not just a technology preference. It is a donor retention strategy.*

*Develop Africa used Network for Good — now known as Bonterra — as a primary donation platform for several years. The service was excellent and the relationship productive. The transition away from it was driven by a specific must-have: the need for a more robust child sponsorship system. Network for Good remains connected to several third-party giving networks, including workplace giving programs, and continues to route some donations to Develop Africa through those channels today.*

*The practical guidance: choose a platform with your must-haves, negotiate for the features you need, and then stay. The cost of switching is always higher than it appears in the moment — not just in setup time, but in donor attrition that you will not always be able to measure.*

Google Doc last saved February 24, 2012. Governance gap exposed. Budget recovers to $110,310.

Dec 2013 Develop Africa joins Google One Today app. Will raise $60,706 in small-dollar donations before app shuts down in 2020.

## PHASE III: STRUCTURAL MATURATION (2014–2018)

2014 First board meeting with real minutes, financial review, and structured deliberation. Governance begins accumulating in practice, not just on paper. Budget: $181,172.

2014 Develop Africa Sierra Leone (DASL) formally registered. Hybrid organizational model established: U.S. 501(c)(3) + Sierra Leone National NGO. Five-member DASL board seated. Rented first Freetown office. 8 local staff.

2014-2016 Ebola crisis. Dream Again Home orphanage established in Wellington in partnership with Door of Hope. 22 children. $30,000 GlobalGiving grant. Significant mission-scope expansion beyond education mandate.

2015 $80K GlobalGiving Ebola grant. Center established for remedial training for pregnant girls excluded from school. Budget: $256,182.

Mar 2017 Second GlobalGiving site visit. Alix Halloran visits Sierra Leone.

Dec 2016 Amadou, a program participant, dies of malaria. Illness over several days. Hospital access not possible in time. Word reaches Sylvester by email from Freetown colleagues.

Aug 2017 DASL board convenes. Structured phase-out of Dream Again Home approved. One-year timeline. Family tracing, reunification counseling, transition packages, microfinance for receiving families.

2018 Phase-out complete. 18 of 21 children placed with families or adopted internationally. Budget: $230,993.

## PHASE IV: INSTITUTIONAL DURABILITY (2019–PRESENT)

May 2019 Third GlobalGiving site visit. Dalila Sumani visits Sierra Leone.

2020 COVID-19. Donations contract. Rent deferral negotiated with landlord. Staff payments delayed. Google One Today shuts down. Organization survives through existing systems. Budget: $223,462.

2021 Recovery. Budget reaches $354,162.

2022 Peak budget: $425,056. Kamawornie nursery school construction begins. Community co-designs and contributes labor.

2022-2024 Three-block nursery school constructed in Kamawornie village. Community members fetch water, supply stones, mold blocks, provide labor. Model of community-led development in practice.

Jun 2024 $50,000 unrestricted COVID recovery grant from GlobalGiving. One of 10 organizations selected globally from the Sector Strengthening cohort.

2024 Kamawornie nursery classroom opens. Sylvester is in Johnson City, Tennessee, looking at photographs. No approval required. Budget: $404,644. Cumulative GlobalGiving total: $857,785.

2025 USAID phase-out. Funding environment more competitive than ever.

Fundraising event: MC walks table to table. $600+ raised in 30 minutes without founder making the ask. Institution stands alone.

2003 to 2025: from a girl on Howe Street to a classroom in Kamawornie — and to 100,000 pencils placed in the hands of 10,000 children on a single day in Freetown.

From a problem one person could not ignore to an institution others can carry.

# Appendix C — Glossary of Frameworks and Models

Mission to Systems™ introduces a set of named frameworks developed from Develop Africa's institutional experience. Each framework is a diagnostic tool, not a prescription. They are listed here in chapter order for reference. Where a framework appears, the relevant chapter is noted.

### Chapter 1 — Mission Definition

## The Problem Compression Model™

A framework for narrowing broad mission energy into a governable, defined core. Problem compression requires an organization to identify the specific population it serves, the specific problem it addresses, the specific intervention it delivers, and the specific change it produces. Without compression, activity expands without alignment. With compression, every decision is filtered through a clearly defined problem statement.

### Chapter 2 — Mission, Vision, and Values

## The Institutional Clarity Framework™

A vertical alignment model showing how problem definition anchors institutional identity. Values regulate behavior. Mission governs present action. Vision directs long-term resolution. When aligned, the institution is stable. When disconnected, fragmentation begins. An organization that cannot explain the relationship between its values, mission, and vision cannot expect its board, staff, or donors to maintain alignment under pressure.

## The Alignment Triangle™

A visual model of the three-way relationship between mission (what we do now), vision (what we are working toward), and values (how we operate in every decision). The triangle fails when any one element is absent, undefined, or contradicted by organizational behavior.

### Chapter 3 — Organizational Structure

## The Structural Fit Model™

A decision framework for evaluating which organizational form — fiscal sponsorship, giving circle, social enterprise, or independent 501(c)(3) — best matches the organization's mission, timeline, capacity, and accountability requirements. Structure should follow demonstrated need and mission fit, not ambition or external pressure.

## Chapter 4 — Legal Formation

# The Formation Discipline Model™

A framework for treating legal formation as an architectural decision rather than an administrative one. Formation discipline requires mission specificity in the articles of incorporation, bylaws that are customized and understood, documented authority boundaries, an active compliance calendar, and a conflict-of-interest policy. Formation is not complete when the paperwork is filed. It is complete when governance is functional.

## Chapter 5 — Board Governance

# The Governance Function Model™

A model distinguishing between boards that exist on paper (ceremonial), boards that attend and respond (engaged), and boards that set policy, review finances, evaluate leadership, and hold distributed authority (governing). Most early-stage nonprofits begin ceremonial. Durability requires reaching governing. The model provides diagnostic language for identifying where a board currently sits and what movement toward governance function requires.

# The Board Governance Spectrum™

A visual representation of the three board states — Ceremonial, Engaged, and Governing — showing the behavioral and structural differences at each stage. Used as a board self-assessment tool and as a framework for governance conversations that are often difficult to initiate without shared language.

## The Authority Distribution Model™

A framework for mapping where decision-making authority resides across the organization — founder, executive director, board, committees, staff. Organizations in which authority is concentrated in a single individual are structurally fragile. Authority distribution is not delegation for its own sake; it is the structural mechanism by which governance becomes real rather than nominal.

### Chapter 6 — Program Integrity

## The Program Integrity Model™

A framework establishing that programs must precede fundraising — that is, a program must be defined, documented, and deliverable before resources are sought to fund it. Programs built on funding opportunity rather than mission clarity produce instability when the funding changes. The model also addresses mission scope discipline: the capacity to distinguish between responding to urgent need and operating within organizational competency.

## Chapter 7 — Financial Systems

# The Financial Credibility Model™

A framework for the relationship between financial transparency and institutional trust. Financial credibility is not a function of budget size. It is a function of explainability: whether any authorized person can explain the organization's financial position clearly and accurately at any time. Organizations in which financial information is held by one person, stored informally, or not reviewed by the board lack financial credibility regardless of their budget.

# The Financial Transparency Stack™

A visual model showing the layered relationship between financial systems: bank account separation, documentation, chart of accounts, expense approval, board financial review, cash-flow forecasting, and external audit. Each layer supports the one above it. Organizations that skip layers expose themselves to compounding risk as budgets grow.

## Chapter 8 — Fundraising Strategy

# The Stage-Aligned Fundraising Model™

A framework matching fundraising strategy to organizational maturity stage. Foundation Stage organizations (under $100K) rely on direct relationship-based giving. Growth Stage organizations ($100K–$500K) add platform diversification and corporate engagement. Mature organizations ($500K+) pursue institutional funding and endowment strategy. The model exists because organizations that pursue fundraising tactics misaligned with their stage produce instability: early-stage organizations chasing institutional grants before systems exist, or mature organizations remaining dependent on individual donors who are irreplaceable.

## Chapter 9 — Operational Systems

# The Operational Continuity Model™

A framework for the relationship between documented systems and organizational continuity. Operational continuity exists when an organization can maintain program delivery, financial processing, donor communication, and governance function without any specific individual. The model identifies the core systems that must be documented — financial processes, program SOPs, reporting workflows, governance structures, and onboarding materials — and the conditions that trigger the realization that continuity has not yet been built.

# The Systemization Flow Map™

A visual model of the process by which informal practices become documented systems: identify the practice, document the sequence, assign ownership, test for reproducibility, and build a review cadence. The map addresses the most common reason organizations fail to build systems: the assumption that documentation is a future task rather than a present discipline.

## Chapter 10 — Governance Maturity

# The Governance Maturity Continuum™

A four-stage model of governance development: Founder-Centric (all authority resides with founder), Structurally Emerging (governance structures exist but are inconsistently practiced), Structured Governance (consistent board cadence, financial review, and executive evaluation), and Institutional Governance (governance is embedded, self-correcting, and founder-independent). The Continuum exists because governance does not arrive fully formed. It accumulates through repeated practice, often under pressure, and usually later than founders recognize.

## Chapter 11 — Impact Measurement

# The Impact Integrity Model™

A framework distinguishing outputs (activities and counts — number of scholarships distributed, number of training participants) from outcomes (measurable changes in the lives of beneficiaries — enrollment rates, exam passage rates, income changes). Impact integrity requires that organizations measure what changed, not only what happened. The model includes a basic M&E framework, a quarterly outcome review process, and an annual impact summary structure.

## Chapter 12 — Scaling and Sustainability

# The Structural Scaling Model™

A framework for evaluating whether an organization is structurally ready to scale before expanding. Scaling without proportional institutional strength produces fracture, not growth. The model assesses governance maturity, SOP documentation, financial forecasting capacity, revenue diversification, leadership delegation, and reporting volume capacity before approving expansion..

# The Scaling Readiness Matrix™

A two-axis visual tool mapping funding availability against systems strength to identify four organizational states: Scale-Ready (strong systems + available funding), High Risk (weak systems + available funding), Build Phase (strong systems + limited funding), and Stable Danger (weak systems + limited funding, where the absence of pressure conceals fragility). The matrix is designed for pre-expansion board discussions.

## Chapter 13 — Founder Risk and Sustainability

## The Founder Continuity Model™ / Founder Continuity Spectrum™

A four-stage model of founder dependency reduction: Stage 1 (Founder as System — all decisions flow through founder), Stage 2 (Founder as Center — most decisions require founder input), Stage 3 (Founder as Architect — systems run without daily founder involvement), Stage 4 (Founder as Steward — board and staff lead daily operations). Most early organizations begin at Stage 1. Durability requires reaching Stage 3 or 4. The model provides language for the founder transition that is often avoided because it feels like abandonment. The Spectrum makes visible that designing oneself out of indispensability is not departure — it is the highest form of stewardship.

These frameworks are diagnostic tools, not compliance requirements. The question is never whether your organization has implemented a framework. It is whether the framework names something real about your current institutional condition — and whether naming it honestly creates the conditions for addressing it.

# Appendix D — Master Decision Checklist and Governance Self-Assessment

The following tools are designed for practical use—not as one-time checklists but as instruments you return to at each stage of organizational development. Apply them honestly. The gaps you identify are not failures. They are starting points.

## If You Only Do 5 Things From This Book

If you implement nothing else, these five actions will most directly shift your organization's structural trajectory:

1. Define your compressed problem clearly—in one sentence

2. Write one program with measurable outcomes

3. Separate finances and document everything

4. Clarify board vs. executive roles in writing

5. Document at least one core process

These five actions address the root causes of structural weakness. Everything else in this book deepens or reinforces them.

## Red Flags: What to Watch For

The following patterns are structural warning signs. They are not character flaws. They are predictable indicators that structure has not kept pace with growth.

> **Red flag:** You cannot take a week off without checking in daily.
>
> This is structural dependency.
>
> **Red flag:** Your board rubber-stamps every decision.
>
> This is governance failure.
>
> **Red flag:** You know every detail of every program.
>
> This is the founder bottleneck.
>
> **Red flag:** New staff quit before they are fully trained.
>
> This is documentation failure.

**Red flag:** Crises happen monthly but no one documents the fixes.

This is pattern avoidance.

## Questions for Self-Assessment

Return to these questions annually—or before any major decision, expansion, or transition:

If you stepped away for 30 days, what would stop?

Can you explain your program's outcomes to a stranger in 60 seconds?

Does your board have the information it needs to review and challenge financial reports?

If the founder left tomorrow, would the organization continue?

Could someone new to your organization run your most critical process?

## Your Implementation Roadmap

Use this checklist to guide your next steps. This is not a one-time exercise. Return to it each time your organization enters a new stage of development.

☐ Define your compressed problem in one sentence

☐ Map one program with clear, measurable outcomes

☐ Separate personal and organizational finances

☐ Write board position descriptions and expectations

☐ Document your three most critical processes

☐ Schedule quarterly governance reviews

☐ Create a founder succession plan

☐ Use this book as your team's study guide

# Systems or Heroes: The Difference Over Time

Organizations built on heroics feel impressive in the moment. A charismatic founder. A tireless fundraiser. A brilliant program director. They create breakthroughs. They feel dynamic.

But they are fragile.

Organizations built on systems look quieter from the outside. Documented processes. Clear roles. Built-in redundancy. From the outside, they might seem less exciting.

But they are durable.

The difference becomes visible over time. The organization built on heroics hits a ceiling—the limit of what one person can carry. The organization built on systems keeps scaling.

This is not a choice between impressive and boring. It is a choice between sustainable and temporary. Choose systems.

## The Danger of Early Success

Early success can mask structural weakness. What works at small scale often fails under pressure. A founder can hold everything in their head when the organization is three people. At fifteen people, the same approach creates chaos.

This is not a failure of the founder. It is a failure to recognize that success at one scale does not equal readiness for the next. The organization that succeeds early without systems often struggles most when it grows.

This is why many successful founders struggle with scaling. Their success masked the need for structure. Their growth revealed it.

## Why Institutional Readiness Matters Globally

When institutions are weak, progress becomes temporary. A program runs because one person drives it. Then that person leaves. The program ends.

When institutions are strong, progress becomes durable. A program survives because the organization survives. It adapts. It evolves. It outlasts its founder.

This distinction matters everywhere—in nonprofit organizations, in development work, in social enterprises, in emerging organizations across Africa, Asia, and Latin America. Institutional readiness is not a nonprofit concern. It is a development imperative.

## This Will Return (At Higher Complexity)

Even after you address structural weakness once, it will return—at a higher level of complexity. You will solve governance at ten people. Then face different governance questions at thirty. Then again at one hundred.

This is not failure. This is evolution. The structure that holds at one scale must evolve at the next. This book prepares you not to solve these problems once, but to recognize and address them each time they return. Each time, you will move faster. Each time, you will be more intentional.

## The Moment of Truth

There will come a moment when everything in this book is tested.

A major funder will ask you to expand. A need in your community will feel urgent. A shortcut will present itself as justified. Growth will feel more important than systems. Speed will seem more valuable than documentation.

In that moment, you will choose between institutional integrity and immediate opportunity. That choice defines whether you are building something to last or something that will break under pressure.

Build so that when that moment comes—and it will—you choose institution over impulse. System over speed. Sustainability over sensation.

### Domain 1: Mission and Program Clarity

Before launching or expanding any program:

☐ The problem the organization addresses is specifically defined
☐ The population served is clearly identified (not broadly described)
☐ The intervention is documented and deliverable before fundraising begins
☐ The outcome — what change is expected — is stated and measurable
☐ The cost of producing that change is known
☐ The program does not rely on founder overextension to operate
☐ Mission clarity has been tested: has it ever been the deciding factor in a hard institutional choice?

If multiple boxes are unchecked: clarify first. Fundraise second.

## Domain 2: Legal Formation and Structure

Before declaring formation complete:

☐ Articles of incorporation reflect mission specificity
☐ Bylaws are customized, understood, and accessible to all board members
☐ Authority boundaries are documented (who can approve what)
☐ Compliance calendar is established (990 deadlines, state filings, renewals)
☐ Conflict-of-interest policy is active and signed annually
☐ Documentation process is standardized and stored centrally
☐ Board understands fiduciary responsibility — not just in concept
☐ Organizational structure chosen matches mission fit, not ambition

If incomplete: formation is cosmetic. Cosmetic structure fails under pressure.

## Domain 3: Board Governance

Before declaring governance stable:

☐ Board size is disciplined (3–7 voting members recommended)
☐ Board member roles are documented and understood
☐ Authority boundaries between board, ED, and staff are defined
☐ Financial oversight is active — board reviews financials at least quarterly
☐ Executive evaluation is formalized and conducted annually
☐ Term limits are defined and enforced
☐ Meeting cadence is consistent and minutes are kept
☐ Conflict-of-interest policy is enforced, not just on file
☐ Succession is discussed openly — not treated as a threatening topic
☐ Board could govern effectively if founder were absent for 60 days

If multiple boxes are unchecked: governance is symbolic. Symbolic governance collapses under pressure.

## Domain 4: Financial Systems

Before declaring financial foundations stable:

☐ Separate organizational bank account established and maintained
☐ Financial documentation is organized, labeled, and accessible

☐ Chart of accounts is structured for the organization's program model
☐ Expense approval process is documented and consistently followed
☐ Board reviews financial statements at least quarterly
☐ Cash-flow forecasting exists and is used for planning decisions
☐ Conflict-of-interest policy is active in financial decision-making
☐ Any authorized person can explain the financial position clearly
☐ Fundraising strategy is aligned with organizational maturity stage

If multiple boxes are unchecked: revenue growth will amplify risk, not stability.

## Domain 5: Operational Systems and Impact

Before declaring operational stability:

☐ Core financial processes are documented as repeatable SOPs
☐ At least one full program SOP exists and is consistently used
☐ Reporting workflows are defined — who produces what, by when, for whom
☐ Governance processes are structured and survive personnel change
☐ Onboarding materials exist for new board members and key staff
☐ Documentation is stored centrally and is findable without the founder
☐ SOP ownership is assigned — each process has a named accountable party
☐ Review cadence exists — SOPs are updated, not just filed

Impact credibility:

☐ Outputs are tracked consistently (activities and counts)
☐ Outcomes are clearly defined (what change is expected)
☐ Baseline data exists for comparison
☐ Measurement tools are simple and repeatable by program staff
☐ Data informs program refinement — not only funder reports
☐ Reports distinguish activity from change
☐ Board reviews outcome data at least annually

If several are missing: growth will strain stability.
If impact items are inconsistent: impact credibility is fragile.

## Domain 6: Scaling Readiness and Founder Continuity

Before approving expansion:

☐ Governance maturity level is stable (Structured or Institutional)
☐ SOP documentation is complete for core processes
☐ Financial forecasting supports proposed growth
☐ Revenue diversification plan exists — not dependent on one source
☐ Leadership roles are clearly delegated with real authority
☐ Reporting capacity can handle increased program volume
☐ A consolidation phase has occurred since the last major expansion

Founder continuity:

☐ The organization could operate for 60 days without the founder
☐ Executive evaluation is formalized annually
☐ Core SOPs are consistently used by staff, not held in founder's memory
☐ Donor communications are scheduled and system-generated, not founder-dependent
☐ Succession is discussed openly at the board level
☐ Authority is distributed to named individuals with clear boundaries
☐ Founder has designed at least one critical function out of personal dependency

Unchecked items indicate structural strain risk.
Expansion without discipline creates volatility.
Expansion with discipline strengthens institutions.

## Governance Maturity Self-Assessment™

Answer candidly. This assessment is most useful when completed by the founder and at least one board member independently, then compared. Discrepancies in answers are themselves governance data.

1. Could the organization operate for 60 days without the founder?
2. Is executive evaluation formalized and conducted annually?
3. Are authority boundaries documented and understood by all parties?
4. Are financial reports actively reviewed by the board (not just received)?
5. Are compliance deadlines calendarized and owned by a named person?

6. Is succession discussed openly — not avoided as threatening?
7. Are core SOPs consistently used, or do they live in one person's practice?
8. Are donor communications predictable, scheduled, and system-driven?

Scoring:
If most answers are "No" → Founder-Centric
If many answers are "Partial" → Structurally Emerging
If most answers are "Yes" → Structured Governance
If consistently embedded → Institutional Governance

Honesty matters more than aspiration.
The stage you are at is not the stage you have to stay at.
But you cannot move from a stage you have not accurately named.

*This appendix is designed to be photocopied, shared with your board, and used as a standing reference. The frameworks and checklists belong to you. The work of implementing them belongs to the organization.*

# Appendix E — Founder Toolkit: Templates & Gate Documents

## Accessing Your Tools

Scan to download all 13 tools at

www.missiontosystems.com/tools

All 13 tools referenced throughout this book are available as **free, downloadable PDFs** at: **www.missiontosystems.com/tools**

You can download these tools individually or as a complete bundle, then print them, fill them out digitally, or share them with your board and leadership team.

---

# THE 13 TOOLS

## Formation & Governance Foundation

**Tool 00: Bylaw Essentials Checklist** Verify that your bylaws address eight critical governance elements before filing incorporation documents. A pre-filing governance framework ensuring structural clarity.

**Tool 01: Mission, Vision & Values Worksheet** Define and align your mission statement, vision, and organizational values. Includes the Mission Discipline Test and Alignment Triangle framework for testing institutional clarity.

**Tool 02: Board Member Agreement** Formalize board expectations before seating a member. Documents fiduciary duties, attendance requirements, fundraising participation, conflict of interest process, and term limits.

**Tool 03: Program One-Pager** Define any program before fundraising. Documents the target population, specific intervention, measurable outcomes, and cost structure in a single page.

## Financial Systems & Operations

**Tool 04: Expense Approval & Documentation SOP** Define tiered approval thresholds, required documentation for transactions, permitted payment methods, the reimbursement process, and record retention schedules aligned with IRS guidelines.

**Tool 05: Founder Role & Boundaries** Document the founder's current responsibilities, formally delegated roles, decision authority boundaries, time boundaries, and support needed. Revisit annually to reduce founder dependency.

**Tool 06: Operating Budget Template** A three-tab workbook covering Revenue, Expenses, and Budget Summary with built-in board narrative prompts. Formula-driven for easy updates and board presentation.

## Board Governance & Leadership

**Tool 07: Board Values Self-Assessment** Move the board's core values from stated commitments to scored behavior. Each member completes individually; scores are aggregated for board-level discussion and alignment.

**Tool 08: Board Orientation & Onboarding Checklist** Ensure every board member is governance-ready before their first vote. Covers mission understanding, role clarity, values and conduct expectations, legal and financial literacy.

**Tool 09: Board Chair Facilitation Guide** Equips the Board Chair to facilitate meetings, handle difficult conversations, and enforce values-based decision rules with clarity and discipline. Includes intervention language and accountability loops.

## Governance Assessment & Strategic Planning

**Tool 10: Governance Maturity Scoring Worksheet** Score the organization across six governance domains with behavioral anchors for levels 1–4. Identifies current maturity stage with recommendations for next actions.

**Tool 11: Governance Maturity 12-Month Roadmap** Translates a Governance Maturity Score into a four-phase,

12-month implementation plan. Links governance priorities to toolkit tools with milestone checkpoints for completion.

### Programs & Impact

**Tool 12: Values-Based Board Decision Rules** Translate organizational values into binding board behavior. Covers Integrity, Accountability, Stewardship, Respect, and Founder Sustainability with clear standards and defined consequences.

**Tool 13: Program Portfolio Dashboard** Evaluate all programs as a portfolio. Includes auto-scored readiness scores (0–100) with traffic-light formatting across six governance dimensions for quarterly leadership review.

---

# HOW TO USE THESE TOOLS

**Step 1: Identify Your Needs** Refer to the chapter(s) most relevant to your organization's current stage. Each chapter recommends specific tools to complete.

**Step 2: Download Tools** Visit **www.missiontosystems.com/tools** and download the tools you need. Tools are available individually or as a complete bundle.

**Step 3: Complete with Your Team** Print tools or fill them out digitally. Many tools are designed for board review or team completion. They are working documents, not one-time exercises.

**Step 4: Revisit Regularly** Most tools are annual or quarterly reviews. Governance Maturity Scoring (Tool 10), for example, should be completed annually to track institutional development.

**Step 5: Adjust & Iterate** The tools are designed to evolve with your organization. As you mature, your answers to these tools will change — that's the point. Track the evolution.

---

# TOOL CUSTOMIZATION

All tools are provided as templates. Customize them to reflect your organization's specific context, governance structure, and stage of institutional development.

Many tools include:

- Blank spaces for your specific language
- Fillable PDF fields for digital completion
- Examples and guidance for each section
- Space for board/team notes and decisions

---

# QUICK REFERENCE: TOOLS BY STAGE

**If you're Founder-Centric (Chapters 1–4):** Start with Tools 00, 01, 02, 03 (Formation & Governance Foundation)

**If you're Structurally Emerging (Chapters 5–9):** Focus on Tools 04, 05, 06, 07, 08 (Financial Systems & Board Governance)

**If you're Structured or Institutional (Chapters 10–13):** Use Tools 10, 11, 12, 13 (Assessment & Strategic Planning)

**For any stage:** Tool 09 (Board Chair Facilitation Guide) is evergreen — relevant regardless of maturity level.

---

# DOWNLOADING & SHARING TOOLS

All tools at www.missiontosystems.com/tools are:

- **Free** to download
- **Shareable** with your board, staff, and partners
- **Printable** for paper-based work
- **Editable** (PDFs can be modified and saved)
- **Available as a bundle** or individually

Tools are updated periodically. Check the website for the most current versions.

---

# SUPPORT & GUIDANCE

Each tool in this appendix is referenced in its corresponding chapter. If you're using a specific tool, refer back to the chapter for:

- Detailed explanation of the tool's purpose
- Step-by-step completion guidance
- Examples from Develop Africa or other organizations
- Common mistakes to avoid
- How to implement findings

---

# NEXT STEPS AFTER READING THIS BOOK

1. **Download and review** the tools most relevant to your current stage
2. **Complete the Governance Maturity Scoring** (Tool 10) to assess where you are
3. **Create a 12-Month Roadmap** (Tool 11) based on your maturity score
4. **Share relevant tools with your board** and schedule completion as part of board workflow
5. **Revisit the applicable chapters** as you implement each tool

The work of institutional development is continuous. These tools provide the structure for that work to be intentional, measurable, and sustainable.

---

# MISSION TO SYSTEMS™: BUILDING INSTITUTIONS THAT ENDURE

The frameworks in this book are built on the principle that mission alone is insufficient. Structure sustains. Systems endure. The tools in this appendix operationalize those frameworks into working practice.

Your mission deserves more than momentum. It deserves architecture.

Use these tools to build it.

---

**For questions, updates, or additional resources, visit www.missiontosystems.com**

# About the Author

Sylvester Renner, MBA, is the Founder and President of Develop Africa, a U.S.-based nonprofit he incorporated on January 30, 2006, to expand access to education and opportunity in Sierra Leone and across underserved communities in Africa.

What began as a computer training program in a modest classroom has grown into an organization with twenty years of documented institutional development — supporting scholarships, school supplies, nursery school construction, and community-based programs across two continents. Develop Africa holds Superstar status on GlobalGiving, has been site-visited by three members of the GlobalGiving team, and has raised over $857,000 through that platform alone.

Sylvester built much of that infrastructure himself — the first website, the early IT systems, the first board structure. He also made many of the mistakes this book is designed to help others avoid: unclear role boundaries, governance that existed on paper before it existed in practice, programs that grew faster than the systems to support them.

Those failures became the framework.

Mission to Systems™: Building Institutions That Endure draws directly from Develop Africa's financial records, governance decisions, and institutional choices across two decades. It is not borrowed theory. It is documented practice.

Sylvester is based in Johnson City, Tennessee. He advises nonprofit founders and boards on institutional development, governance maturity, and sustainable scaling. The programs documented in this book served individual children in Freetown, supported a mother's small business on Lewis Street, refurbished a building in Wellington that housed twenty-two Ebola orphans, constructed a nursery school in rural Kamawornie, and delivered 100,000 pencils to 10,000 children in a single day in partnership with the Mayor of Freetown. These are not isolated wins. They are what sustained institutional presence — governed, documented, and accountable — makes possible across twenty years. The global development sector needs more organizations that can show this kind of arc. This book exists to help build them. Fifteen percent of royalties from every copy of this book sold support student scholarships through Develop Africa in Sierra Leone.

**www.missiontosystems.com | sylrenner.com**

# A Note from Sylvester

*"I didn't start with systems. I started with a mission.*

*Like many founders, I believed that passion, commitment, and hard work would be enough.*

*But over time, I learned that without structure, even the strongest mission begins to strain under its own weight.*

That mission began in 2003, with a girl I passed on Howe Street in Freetown — crouching on the pavement, asking strangers for food. I could not solve poverty. But I could do something specific: help children in Sierra Leone stay in school. Develop Africa was incorporated three years later, on January 30, 2006.

A word about technology — because it is part of the story this book does not tell directly but could not exist without. From the earliest days of Develop Africa, comfort with technology has been a force multiplier. I built the organization's first website myself. I ran network cabling through the drop ceiling of our Johnson City office. I assigned IP addresses to network printers, managed mail merges for donor acknowledgments, and printed thousands of mailing labels. None of this is remarkable in isolation. But in a resource-constrained nonprofit where every dollar spent on outside help is a dollar not spent on programs, the ability to do these things internally was a significant operational advantage. That mindset — I can learn this, I can figure this out — is what led me to every digital platform that has contributed to Develop Africa's sustainability, from UniversalGiving in 2006 to GlobalGiving in 2008 to Google One Today in 2013. For founders starting today, this applies with even greater urgency. The organizations that engage with new technologies early — that develop the institutional habit of learning before tools become standard — will have a structural advantage over those that wait. The willingness to learn is itself a governance asset.

*This book is not theory. It is what I learned — often the hard way — about building something that lasts.*

*My hope is that it helps you move faster, avoid costly mistakes, and build an organization that outlives you. Fifteen percent of royalties from every copy sold support student scholarships through Develop Africa in Sierra Leone. The mission this book came from continues."*

www.ingramcontent.com/pod-product-compliance
Lightning Source LLC
LaVergne TN
LVHW010632110826
845149LV00014B/2831
* 9 7 8 0 9 8 6 0 2 3 0 5 7 *